With a Bible in My Hand

W. A. Criswell

WITH A BIBLE IN MY HAND

Broadman Press
Nashville, Tennessee

Dewey Decimal Classification: 252
Subject heading: SERMONS

Library of Congress Catalog Card Number: 78–69708
Printed in the United States of America

Dedication

To the man of God anywhere in the
earth who stands proclaiming the truth of
Christ *with a Bible in his hand*

Foreword

So these are my favorite sermons! As I look at them and reread them after these fifty years of preaching, they bring back to my heart a thousand precious memories. These are the sermons that I have delivered over and over again. These are the sermons that I have preached since I was a seventeen-year-old boy. These are the sermons that God has blessed to the saving of hundreds of souls.

It is a strange thing how the heart and mind work. I minister to the same congregation year after year—now thirty-five years to the people of the church here in Dallas. I study and prepare my sermons week by week, spending long hours in their preparation. I expound the Word of the Lord, chapter by chapter, verse by verse, book by book. Yet in a revival meeting or in a special conference, there are certain sermons to which I return time after time, year after year. Inevitably they are sermons that sum up my own personal experience in Christ.

While choosing these sixteen sermons as my favorites, I was amazed at a common characteristic they all possess. Without exception, they are everyone eminently and preeminently evangelistic. I started out that way, preaching revivals under tabernacles and arbors and anywhere else anybody would listen to me. My whole heart is still in that soul-winning appeal. It is the soul-winning sermon that most deeply moves my heart. After the apostle

Paul said, "Preach the word," he added to it, "do the work of an evangelist, make full proof of thy ministry" (2 Tim. 4:5). Every pastor ought to heed that apostolic admonition. With all our other and heavy responsibilities, we must never neglect our soul-winning assignment. Winning souls will keep our hearts warm, and it will keep the fires burning in the churches over which God has made us overseers (Acts 20:28). In this must be the reason why my favorite sermons are all evangelistic.

As you read them you will plainly see that they are publicly delivered messages. They were not written out. The words were first heard and then were prepared for publication. They are not essays. They are not speculative discussions. They are proclamations of the good news. They are invitations to accept Jesus as Savior. They are appeals that we become Christians and that we follow the glory road of Jesus to heaven and to home. Oh, that God would use them to convert others to the living, saving faith! It would be worth it all, a thousand times over again, if just one lost soul could find Christ as his personal Savior through these printed pages.

When I began to preach at the age of seventeen, I knelt down before the Lord God and asked him to help me deliver the message "with just a Bible in my hand." I asked for his mercy and his remembrance and his help to preach without notes. It terrified me at first. What if I should forget? And all those people out there, looking at me in my stammering stupidity, unable to continue my sermon because I had forgotten the second point or the poem or the reference in the Holy Scriptures. But the Lord has never let me down. For these fifty years now I have preached "with just a Bible in my hand," and I have never failed to remember the prepared message I studied and prayed to deliver. Speaking extemporaneously, I find the words are not as elegant and the sentences are not as chaste as if they were carefully written out, but they have my heart and soul in them, and that is better. If I were to talk to a man about accepting Jesus as his Savior, I would not sit before him or by his side, reading a manuscript. I would talk to him face to face, heart to heart. It is no different with a congregation. When I am pleading for faith in the risen Christ, let me do it face to face, heart to heart, soul to soul, as if the whole throng were just one lost, prodigal boy.

But enough. May the Holy Spirit of conviction and conversion bless the eyes that look upon these pages and read these oft-preached, favorite sermons. May it be as though I stood before you, pleading, "with a Bible in my hand." God love you; God bless you; God save and keep us all. Amen.

W. A. CRISWELL

First Baptist Church
Dallas, Texas

About the Author

Dr. W. A. Criswell is now celebrating his golden anniversary in the gospel ministry. He has served as pastor of the First Baptist Church, Dallas, Texas, since 1944, when he succeeded the late George W. Truett. Under Dr. Criswell's leadership, the church has grown to more than 20,000 members—and continues to grow.

Dr. Criswell was born in Eldorado, Oklahoma, and grew up in New Mexico. He entered the ministry in 1928 and was a student pastor during college and seminary. He is a graduate of Baylor University and Southern Baptist Seminary. He was also given an honorary degree by Baylor.

He served two years as president of the Southern Baptist Convention. He is the author of almost thirty books, eight by Broadman.

Contents

1.

The Urgency of the Hour

A prayer of Habakkuk the prophet upon Shigionoth.

O Lord, I have heard thy speech, and was afraid: O Lord, revive thy work in the midst of the years, in the midst of the years make known; in wrath remember mercy (Hab. 3:1–2).

This message is entitled, "The Urgency of the Hour" or "Our Greatest Need" or "This Is Revival." The sermon is taken out of the first two verses of the third chapter of Habakkuk.

Of what is the prophet afraid when he says, "O Lord, I have heard thy speech, and was afraid"? He is referring to the judgments of God upon Israel. As the author of Hebrews avows, "It is a fearful thing to fall into the hands of the living God" (Heb. 10:31). The prophet in his fear is referring to the destruction of Israel, the Northern Kingdom of Samaria, in 722 B.C. by the Assyrians, and he is referring to the destruction of Jerusalem and Judah by the Babylonians in 587 B.C. Habakkuk lived during the period between the two events. The first destruction had come to pass, and Habakkuk himself was the emissary and messenger of God to announce the second judgment. That is why he says, "O Lord, I have heard thy speech, and was afraid." He feared the judgment of God that the Lord sent him to announce against his own people and his own city. We read in the first chapter of Habakkuk the Lord's warning concerning the

coming Chaldean captivity that the prophet himself was
called upon to deliver:

> Lo, I raise up the Chaldeans [the Babylonians],
> that bitter and hasty nation, which shall march
> through the breadth of the land, to possess the
> dwellingplaces that are not theirs.
> They are terrible and dreadful: their judgment and
> their dignity shall proceed of themselves.
> Their horses also are swifter than the leopards,
> and are more fierce than the evening wolves: and
> their horsemen shall come from far; they shall fly
> as the eagle that hasteth to eat.
> They shall come all for violence: their faces shall
> sup up as the east wind, and they shall gather the
> captivity as the sand.
> And they shall scoff at the kings, and the princes
> shall be a scorn unto them: they shall deride every
> strong hold; for they shall heap dust, and take it
> (Hab. 1:6–10).

Habakkuk's Question and the Lord's Answer

Habakkuk asks a question of the Lord when he is sent
to announce that his own people would be destroyed
by Babylonia and carried into captivity. He asks: "Lord,
however evil and wicked we may be, we are not more
evil and wicked than the Babylonians. Why do you allow
them to destroy us?" We read Habakkuk's words: "Thou
art of purer eyes than to behold evil, and canst not look
on iniquity: wherefore lookest thou upon them that deal
treacherously, and holdest thy tongue when the wicked
devoureth the man that is more righteous than he?"

The answer comes from God in the twelfth verse: "O
Lord, thou hast ordained them for judgment; and, O

mighty God, thou hast established them for correction" (Hab. 1:12). As Isaiah declared, "O Assyrian, the rod of mine anger, and the staff in their hand is mine indignation" (10:5).

That is the message of God to America today. We cannot continue in drunkenness, debauchery, blasphemy, and desecration and not face the inevitable judgment of Almighty God. The Lord will raise up even these bitter and atheistic Communist nations to chasten us. It is hard for us to realize that America could be lost, that our nation could be destroyed, and that we could be confronted by implacable and ruthless enemies, but that is an imponderable in the hands of Almighty God. Whether we live or die lies in the sovereign judgments of the Judge of all the nations.

Habakkuk's Prayer

Then the prophet gave himself to the one recourse that is possible for us. Habakkuk prayed, ". . . O Lord, revive thy work in the midst of the years, in the midst of the years make known; in wrath remember mercy" (Hab. 3:2). Revival will save a nation. It saved Judah in the days of Hezekiah. It saved England in the days of the Wesleys. Revival will save a city. It saved Nineveh in the days of Jonah. It saved Antioch in the days of John Chrysostom. It saved Florence, Italy, in the days of Savonarola. Revival will save a home; it will save a life. It did yesterday; it does today; and it will forever.

What Is Revival?

Revival is a Christian word. It is a family word. The lost are not revived. They are dead in trespasses and in sin. The lost need to be resurrected. They need to be born again. They need life out of death. It is the Christian people, the family of God who are to be revived.

Revival is a church word. It is an assembly word. As Peter writes in the fourth chapter of his first epistle, "For the time is come that judgment must begin at the house of God" (v. 17). The church can never give what it does not possess. There first must be in the church the presence of the Lord and all the joy and gladness that pertain to the bountiful goodnesses of God. The overflowing, abounding presence of the Spirit of God is revival.

Revival is a normal word. We are not straining after some monstrous experience alien to the mind of God. But we are turning our hearts and hands upward to receive from God's gracious goodness all of the bountiful and heavenly blessing that he has for us who love him. Revival is a normal word.

What would you think of a father whose children were sick and in bed all year long, and the father says: "But do not worry. Let it be of no concern or burden to you. You see, next year my children will be up for another week"? Such an experience is unthinkable, that one's children would only be up for one week out of the year. The same is true of God's children. Our lives are to be overflowing with joy, gladness, and praise every day of the week. The church is to be quickened with the presence, the power, and the Spirit of God. Revival is a normal word.

But how can we live upwardly, triumphantly, blessedly the life of a revived, quickened soul?

Revival Comes in the Spirit
of Contrition and Confession

Revival comes first by confession and contrition. "O God, forgive my stubborn pride, forgive my sterile unfruitfulness, forgive my lack of burden." We may be praying because we cannot pray, weeping because we cannot weep, burdened because we are not burdened. We may become full of concern and care because we are indifferent. We need to recognize and confess our hardness of heart. Revival comes when believers with sobbing souls turn back to Calvary. That is the beginning of real revival—

Revival Comes in the Spirit
of Travail and Agony in Prayer

Isaiah said:

> Behold, the Lord's hand is not shortened, that it cannot save; neither his ear heavy, that it cannot hear:
> But your iniquities have separated between you and your God, and your sins have hid his face from you, that he will not hear (59:1–2).

That is why in the old-time church they had the mourner's bench. It is not easy to forsake sin. It is not easy to deny the flesh. It is not easy to live the revived and victorious life. We must confess our sins unto God before whose eyes our very souls are ever open and naked. We must pray in burden for the lost. It must be a care and a concern to us whether people are saved or lost. Paul began Romans 9 with this word: "I have great heaviness and continual sorrow in my heart. For I could wish that myself were accursed from Christ for my brethren, my kinsmen according to the flesh" (vv. 2–3). He began the tenth chapter of Romans in the same way: "Brethren, my heart's desire and prayer to God for Israel is, that they might be saved" (v. 1).

It is not revival when we go through the days of the

week and never think of the lost who are all around us. It is not revival when we come into the assembly of the church of the living God and it is no burden to us whether the people respond to the invitation to accept Christ or not. Revival is a burden for the lost that they might be saved.

Revival Is a Spirit of Unity or Oneness, of Togetherness in the Lord

The great Pentecostal chapter in Acts 2:1 begins: "When the day of Pentecost was fully come, they were all with one accord in one place." There was no divisive spirit among them, but they were all given to one great dedication. That is revival in the church.

One time I looked through a magazine and followed a series of pictures of one of the saddest stories that one could imagine. The first picture was of a vast wheat field in Western Kansas. From horizon to horizon, as far as the eye could see, the field was covered with wheat.

The second picture was of the distress of the mother who was in a farmhouse in the middle of the wheat field. She had a small boy who somehow had wandered away from the house into the wheat field. She could not find him, so she called for her husband, and they searched for the lad. They finally called for the neighbors who all began looking. They searched through that illimitable field for the little boy, but they could not find him.

The next picture depicted all of the people who heard of that little boy being lost, joining hands in a great sweep as they said: "Let us join hands and let us go through this wheat field and comb it from one side to the other until we find that little boy."

The last picture would break one's heart. It was a picture of the father standing over the body of his little boy. They had finally found him, but the lad was dead. Underneath the picture were the words of the father as he cried, "O God, that we had joined hands before!" One could not forget a story like that.

Revival in the church means that in the hearts of the people there is a true unity in intercession, always the spirit of seeking and searching, always that seeking note.

Revival Is the Spirit of Longing and Hungering for God

True revival is ever accompanied by a hungering and a thirsting after God. David in the book of Psalms says, "O God, thou art my God; early will I seek thee: my soul thirsteth for thee, my flesh longeth for thee in a dry and thirsty land" (63:1). David also says in Psalms 42:1: "As the hart panteth after the water brooks, so panteth my soul after thee, O God." There is a profound meaning in that passage to those who have found the Lord.

Have you drunk of the water of this life and still thirst? Have you found the emptiness of the rewards of the world? Is there still a longing in your heart for something more than the flesh and the world could afford? You will find it in God, not in the world.

Robert Burns wrote it like this:

> But pleasures are like poppies spread,
> You seize the flow'r, its bloom is shed;
> Or like the snow-falls in the river,
> A moment white—then melts for ever;
> Or like the borealis race
> That flit ere you can point their place;
> Or like the rainbow's lovely form
> Evanishing amid the storm.

How empty and fleeting are the pleasure and rewards of this world!

Hymn writer Leila M. Morris said it like this:

If you are tired of the load of your sin,
Let Jesus come into your heart;
If you desire a new life to begin,
Let Jesus come into your heart.

Just now, your doubtings give o'er;
Just now, reject him no more;
Just now, throw open the door;
Let Jesus come into your heart.

Revival Is the Spirit of Response and Commitment

Revival is the spirit of affirmation, response, and commitment. As a man said to me: "Preacher, I have said no to God for the last time, I am coming to Jesus."

The spirit of rejection? No. The spirit of unbelief? No. The spirit of affirmation? Yes. The spirit of answering God's call? Yes. The spirit of commitment? Yes. "Lord, I am coming." I have decided to follow Jesus.

I am resolved no longer to linger,
Charmed by the world's delight;
Things that are higher, things that are nobler,
These have allured my sight.
. . . .
I am resolved, and who will go with me?
Come, friends, without delay,
Taught by the Bible, led by the Spirit,
We'll walk the heav'nly way.

PALMER HARTSOUGH

2.
What Must I Do
to Be Saved?

*Then he . . . brought them out, and said, Sirs, what must I do
to be saved?*

*And they said, Believe on the Lord Jesus Christ, and thou shalt
be saved, and thy house (Acts 16:29–31).*

The passage of Scripture in our text is the only place
in the Bible where the question is directly asked, "What
must I do to be saved?" and directly answered, "Believe
on the Lord Jesus Christ, and thou shalt be saved."

The jailer was responsible with his own life for the
prisoners. When he thought that they had escaped, rather
than face disgrace and execution in a Roman trial, he
drew out his sword to plunge it through his own heart.
When Paul saw that he was about to take his life, he
cried, saying: "No, no, not one of us has escaped. We
are all here, all of us." Upon that plea from Paul, the
jailer, having heard the message of Paul as he preached
in the city of Philippi, came before him, and in repentance
and contrition fell down before the apostles and asked
that crying question, "What must I do to be saved?"

Why Must a Man Be Saved?

First, why must a man be saved? The answer to the
Philippian jailer was because of the imminent peril of
death, and that is our reply also. It is because of the
imminency of death in every life that we need to be

saved. The second chapter of the book of Genesis tells us: "In the day that thou eatest thereof, thou shalt surely die" (v. 17). God has welded together that link of sin and death in an unbroken chain.

In the prophecy of Ezekiel we read, "the soul that sinneth, it shall die" (Ezek. 18:4). Romans 6:23 says, "For the wages of sin is death." Sin and judgment, sin and death always go together. Physical death, moral death, spiritual death, the second death, eternal death—to sin is to die. There is no escape. All of us face that inevitable penalty like this jailer. The tragedy of all life and all living is this: Somewhere, sometime we all shall face inexorable and inevitable death.

One time I heard of a man who was condemned for a crime that he had not committed. It was in the days of Queen Victoria. The man was sentenced for life in the penitentiary. On the outside of the penitentiary he had a friend who, knowing that the man had been condemned unjustly, worked through the years for his freedom and pardon.

Finally, before Queen Victoria herself, the friend made appeal. He won his case and Queen Victoria signed the pardon for the man.

With gladness and joy he went to the prison, was taken to the cell where his friend had been incarcerated for most of his life, and said: "Look, I have your pardon. You are a free man. You can walk out in liberty and freedom. Your pardon has been signed by the Queen herself!"

The man gave no response, no recognition, no appreciation whatsoever. His friend said: "It must have been that you have been in prison so long that you do not realize, but I have your pardon. You are a free man. You can walk out of this penitentiary in freedom!"

In a piteous, tragic way, the prisoner pulled apart the garments that clothed his breast and exhibited to his dear friend who had worked for his freedom a large, ugly, eating cancer. In sadness, the prisoner looked into the face of the friend and said, "Go ask the Queen if she can heal this."

We are all that way. We have liberty; that is, we have liberty to die. We have length of days; that is, we have length of days to die. We grow old; that is, we grow old to die. We have life; that is, we have life to die. "It is appointed unto men once to die," and we shall inevitably face somewhere, sometime that inexorable hour.

Why does a man need to be saved? Because of the judgment of death upon his sin.

When Should a Man Be Saved?

Second, when is it that a man ought to be saved? The Word of God always pleads and answers with one word, just as Paul would have said to that tragic and condemned jailer. The word is "Now." God's Word never says "Tomorrow." No apostle ever preached, "Some more convenient time," or, "Some other day." The answer from God to the question of when a man should be saved is always, "Now," such as we read in 2 Corinthians 6:2: "Behold, now is the accepted time; behold, now is the day of salvation." When should a man be saved? It is now. There are truths in our lives that argue for that decision and that commitment.

One is the uncertainty of life. I have no mortgage on any tomorrow. I may be in God's presence before the sun rises in the morning. Some tragic accident may take my life away any moment, any time, or I may be felled with a tragic seizure or heart attack. There is no one of us who knows what any tomorrow may bring. The uncer-

tainties of life plead "Now." Nor is that plea made only
to men and women of age. Young people also face that
inexorable judgment and death.

Well can I remember pleading with a young fellow
fifteen years of age to accept Christ. *He was young; he had
time.* He said to me, "Soon I will do it, but not now."
He left me without responding to the Lord. The next
time I saw him, not long after, I stood in a hospital room
over his unconscious body. The doctor turned his face
to me and said, "The boy is gone." He died without
God, without Christ, and without hope. The uncertainties
of life plead that *now* is the time to give your heart to
Jesus.

The usefulness of life pleads with a man to be saved
now. What we offer to God should not be a husk, not
a shell, not a remnant, not a piece, not the end of a
wretched life but the whole life, the whole soul, and
the whole heart. The blessedness and usefulness of life,
all that life means, we should dedicate to God in its fullness now.

When I was a youth pastoring a country church in a
county-seat town in Texas, there was a precious and
beautiful girl married to a young man. Into their home
came two darling little girls. In a providence cruel and
dark, the cause of which I do not remember, he left and
went out into the world. The man left the little mother
and those two baby girls.

What she did was, she went to the edge of town, rented
the cheapest home that she could find, and took in washing. For years of her life, she poured herself into the
caring for those two little girls and rearing them up in
the love of Jesus. She provided piano lessons for them
and all of the other things by which she did her utmost
in the toil of her hands to rear those two little girls.

On a day when the girls were grown, a man came to their cottage and knocked at the door. When she opened the door, she looked at him. He had aged and his years of sin had made deep, indelible marks in his face. It was her husband. As he stood there at the door, diseased and wretched, he asked if he could come in and if she would take him back. To the amazement of the people of the community, she opened wide her door, she opened her arms, and took him back. She cared for him until he died—a beautiful, commendable, and precious response on the part of the wife.

But there is not a man of judgment and fairness who would but say that what the father of those children and the husband of that wife did was a heinous, sorrowful, and tragic thing. That is what happens when a man gives his life to the world, devotes the strength of his days to sin, and then he comes to God before he dies and offers to the Lord a husk, a remnant, a piece. It is not right.

The usefulness of life pleads with a man to give himself to God now, that he be saved now. Not only does one enjoy the fullness and the blessedness of life, but it is great to be a Christian boy or a Christian girl. It is no less marvelous to be a Christian man or a Christian woman. It is precious to have a Christian home and a Christian family as it is wonderful beyond words of description to die in a Christian faith and in a Christian commitment. When should a man be saved? Now!

How Can a Man Be Saved?

What must I do to be saved? "Believe on the Lord Jesus Christ, and thou shalt be saved." First, that is one thing and not two things. It is not "Believe and be baptized, and thou shalt be saved." It is not "Believe and

take the Lord's Supper, and thou shalt be saved." It is
not "Believe and join the church, and thou shalt be
saved." It is not even "Believe and do good works, and
thou shalt be saved." It is one thing and that alone. "Believe on the Lord Jesus Christ, and thou shalt be saved."
That is the eternal plan of salvation through the unending
ages. It is always one thing, one alone.

In the Gospel of John our Lord said: "As Moses lifted
up the serpent in the wilderness, even so must the Son
of man be lifted up: That whosoever believeth in him
should not perish, but have eternal life" (3:14–15). When
a man was stricken and faced inevitable death by the
bite of those sinister, sinuous serpents, all he had to do
to be saved was to look and live. Less could not have
been asked, and more by some could not have been
offered.

"Look and live," my brother, live,
Look to Jesus now and live;
'Tis recorded in His Word, Hallelujah!
It is only that you "look and live."

W. A. OGDEN

Believe and be saved. Always it is one thing and not
two.

Second, salvation is a gift from God and not a prize
that we win. Eternal life is free from God; it is not something we earn. A heavenly home is a gift from God; it
is not a reward of our works. A man does not buy salvation with money. It is not for sale. One does not attempt
to be good enough to deserve it. How could one ever
be worth the atoning death of the Son of God? Nor is
a man able to be astute enough to achieve salvation. Ever-

lasting salvation is something that God does for us. If it were a matter of money to buy our salvation, some of us might be too poor to buy it. If it were a matter of virtue and work, some of us might be too steeped in sin ever to achieve it. If it were a matter of education, some of us might be too unlearned ever to know it.

It is in God's goodness, grace, pity, and mercy that he wrote on the sacred page: "For by grace [unmerited favor] are ye saved through faith; and not that of yourselves: it is the gift of God: Not of works, lest any man should boast" (Eph. 2:8–9). Never am I able to earn it or achieve it. Only God is able to save me. When I die and am buried in the heart of the earth, it must be God who speaks me to life. Likewise, it must be God in his grace who stands by my side when I appear before the judgment bar of the great Judge of all the earth. Salvation is a gift of God, and it is not something that I earn.

Last, salvation is an act of commitment and not a human speculation. It is an act of trust. It is not words of an argument. It is a commitment to Jesus my Lord. It is a hope; it is a faith; it is a trust. You say, "But how unusual!" No. That is the reason God did it that way. That is the way we live.

All life is lived by faith, all of it. When I go to the bank and make a deposit, I thereby trust in the bank and commit what I might have to their safekeeping. When I write a letter and I mail it, I am thereby trusting the post office to take care of the letter and to deliver it. When I board an airplane, it is by faith that I ride in the plane trusting the pilot. I am absolutely helpless. I know nothing about flying a plane. I just sit there trusting in the pilot. When I make a payment on an insurance policy, I am trusting the company that when I die, they will be faithful to that contract and commitment. When

I drive down the highway and over every bridge, I do not get out and examine the bridge. I just drive over the bridge, trusting the highway department that they built the bridge properly. When I eat a meal, it could be poisoned. I trust those who have prepared it.

What I give to others can I not give to Christ? If I trust a pilot, a post office, an insurance company, a bank, a bridge, or people who can the foods that I eat, do I stagger before trusting Jesus my Lord? Cannot I trust him to keep his word, to keep his promise, to save my soul, to stand by me in life, to be by me in death, and to be my Intercessor, Mediator, and Savior in the world that is to come? Salvation is an act of faith and committal. But I must make that act and I must offer that committal, or I cannot be saved.

In the days of the Passover, anyone who was under the blood was saved, but he had to be under the blood. The woman who was so tragically afflicted with an issue of blood touched the hem of Jesus' garment and was healed, but she had to touch the hem of his garment. The thief, repentant on the cross, only turned his head and said, "Lord, remember me," and was saved, but he had to turn his head and say, "Lord, remember me." Romans 10:13 avows: "Whosoever shall call upon the name of the Lord shall be saved," but we must call. Salvation always follows an act of faith. Romans 10:9–10 defined it like this:

> If thou shalt confess with thy mouth the Lord Jesus, and shalt believe in thine heart that God hath raised him from the dead, thou shalt be saved. For with the heart man believeth unto righteousness; and with the mouth confession is made unto salvation.

The Lord said it like this in Matthew: "Whosoever therefore shall confess me before men, him will I confess also before my Father which is in heaven" (10:32). That act of faith is the open, public, unashamed commitment of my life to Jesus. I take him as my Savior. So help me God, here I stand. That is the open door into the kingdom!

3.
The Way Made Plain

Then Philip opened his mouth, and began at the same scripture, and preached unto him Jesus (Acts 8:35).

The story in our text is one of the most poignant of all of the conversions that are described in the Bible.

One of the attendant evils of the Oriental harem was the ever-present eunuch. The man in our text was a victim of that terrible institution. He was an emasculated man, a withered branch, a dry stick. He was without hope of issue, posterity, or family. But he must have been a most gifted man, because even though he was a eunuch, he was the treasurer of the state. We would call him the Secretary of the Treasury in America. In England he would be called the Chancellor of the Exchequer. He was the treasurer of the ancient nation of Ethiopia under Candace the Queen. He must have had a wonderful conversion to the truth. Somehow he was a convert to the one and only God. Coming to Jerusalem to worship, he had found a scroll of the prophet Isaiah. As he returned in his chariot to the capital of Ethiopia, he was reading aloud the fifty-third chapter of Isaiah.

The Lord was merciful to this eunuch. He had sent Philip the evangelist down into the desert to stand by the roadside that goes through Gaza. When the chariot came by with the attendant driving the horses and the treasurer sitting in the chariot reading aloud the fifty-

third chapter of Isaiah, the Holy Spirit said to the evangelist, "Join thyself to the chariot." When the Ethiopian
eunuch invited Philip to come and sit with him, he was
reading that passage that describes the blessed Jesus:

> All we like sheep have gone astray; we have
> turned every one to his own way; and the Lord hath
> laid on him the iniquity of us all.
> . . . And who shall declare his generation? for
> he was cut off out of the land of the living (Isa.
> 53:6,8).

The eunuch turned to the evangelist and said:

> I pray thee, of whom speaketh the prophet this?
> of himself, or of some other man? Then Philip
> opened his mouth, and began at the same scripture,
> and preached unto him Jesus (Acts 8:34–35).

There are some wonderful truths revealed to us in that
simple avowal.

The Gospel Message Is the Preaching of Jesus

First, the gospel message is the simple story of Jesus.
Paul describes what the gospel is as he says:

> Moreover, brethren, I declare unto you the gospel
> which I preached unto you, which also ye have re-
> ceived, and wherein ye stand;
> By which also ye are saved, if ye keep in memory
> what I preached unto you, unless ye have believed
> in vain.
> For I delivered unto you first of all that which I

also received, how that Christ died for our sins according to the scriptures;

And that he was buried, and that he rose again
the third day according to the scriptures (1 Cor. 15:1–
4).

The Gospel is the simple story of Jesus. If we send a
missionary across the sea, and he preaches the gospel,
what does he preach? He preaches about Jesus. If a man
stands in the pulpit and after the service is over, one
goes out the door and says, "That preacher preaches the
gospel," what does he mean? He means that the preacher
preaches Jesus. The gospel is the story of the Lord Jesus—
Jesus, born of a virgin; Jesus, going about in his ministry
doing good; Jesus, dying on the cross for our sins; Jesus,
buried in the tomb; the third day, Jesus, raised from
among the dead; forty days later, Jesus, ascending up
into heaven; Jesus, at the right hand of God; and some
triumphant golden tomorrow, Jesus, coming again. That
is what you preach when you preach the gospel. "Philip
opened his mouth, and began at the same scripture, and
preached unto him Jesus" (Acts 8:35).

I heard of a city preacher who was learned, gifted,
and educated. Sunday by Sunday he brought messages
to his rich and fashionable congregation concerning all
of the things of academia, literature, economics, philoso-
phy, and science. One day a little girl came to his office
at the church and said that her mother had sent for him
because she was sick and dying. Would he come and
tell her how to die? The pastor demurred, for he found
that the child lived in the tenement area of the great
city.

The little child was so insistent that her mother had
sent her that finally, acquiescing, he followed the child

down into the slums of the great city, to a certain tenement building, up all of those stairways into a darkened
room where on a bed lay a dying woman. He took his
place by her side and said: "You have sent for me. What
can I do?" The mother replied: "I cannot live. I am dying,
and I am not ready. Will you tell me how to die? Would
you tell me how to meet God? Would you tell me how
I can be saved?"

That fashionable preacher, who, for the years in his
pulpit had spoken of philosophies and high intellectual
speculations, began to speak to her in the terms, in the
language, and in the thought by which he had been
preaching throughout the years. The poor woman, with
deepening disappointment, could not even understand
the nomenclature which he used, much less what he was
talking about. The preacher bowed his head and cried,
"O God, help me." When he prayed, there came back
to his heart the memory of his godly mother and how
she had taught him as a little child the simple story of
Jesus. Then the preacher began to tell the dying woman
about Jesus, how we were lost and Jesus came down
from heaven to teach us the way; how he died for our
sins, and how he was raised and ascended back to glory;
and that he is waiting there for those who put their trust
in him. When he began to talk about Jesus, explaining
the simple story of the Lord, of how if we trust in him
he will save us and about how he is waiting now to
receive us, she began to nod her head. "Oh, yes," she
said, "I can trust a Savior like that."

Do you know what happened? The next Lord's Day
he stood up in his fashionable pulpit and, before all of
those people in the city, he described to them what had
happened the week before. He ended the explanation
with this sentence: "My dear people, I want you to know,

I got that woman into the kingdom of heaven that day, but what is more, I got in myself." That is the gospel, and however we may exegete, expound, and preach about it, the heart and the core of the gospel message is always the simple story of Jesus. "And he preached unto him Jesus."

The Plan of Salvation Is Trusting Jesus

Not only is the gospel message the simple story of Jesus, but the way of salvation is the plain and simple way of trusting Jesus.

One time I went through the whole Bible and underscored wherever in the Bible God tells a man how to be saved. When I had finished going through the Bible, I looked at all the passages that I had marked and was astonished to behold a certain fact. Wherever in the Bible God tells a man how to be saved, he always does it in one simple, monosyllabic sentence. For example, in John 1 we read: "He came unto his own, and his own received him not. But as many as received him, to them gave he power to become the sons of God, even to them that believe on his name" (vv. 11–12). One simple sentence tells us how to be saved.

Again, in John 3 we read: "And as Moses lifted up the serpent in the wilderness, even so must the Son of man be lifted up: That whosoever believeth in him should not perish, but have eternal life" (vv. 14–15). One simple sentence.

The next sentence telling us how to be saved is the most famous sentence in human literature, the most preciously meaningful, John 3:16: "For God so loved the world, that he gave his only begotten Son, that whosoever believeth in him should not perish, but have everlasting life." One simple sentence.

In the fifth chapter of John we read: "Verily, verily, I say unto you, He that heareth my word, and believeth on him that sent me, hath everlasting life, and shall not come into condemnation; but is passed from death unto life" (v. 24).

One simple sentence tells us how to be saved.

In Romans 10 we are told:

> If thou shalt confess with thy mouth the Lord Jesus, and shalt believe in thine heart that God hath raised him from the dead, thou shalt be saved.
>
> For with the heart man believeth unto righteousness; and with the mouth confession is made unto salvation (vv. 9–10).

The plan of salvation is presented again in one simple sentence. When a man comes down the aisle and openly confesses his faith in the Lord Jesus, he is saved. There is no exception to that. Wherever God tells us how to be saved, he will always do it in one simple sentence.

Somebody sent word to a dear preacher friend of mine, saying: "There is a thirteen-year-old boy in the hospital who is dying. Would you go tell him how to be saved?"

The pastor went to the hospital to the room of the boy who was under an oxygen tent. The preacher asked the nurse if he could speak to the boy. The nurse kindly said yes.

The preacher put his head under the oxygen tent with the boy and said, "Son, they tell me that you know that you are not going to live."

"That is right; I am going to die," the boy replied.

Then the pastor said, "They tell me that you are not a Christian—you are not saved."

"That is right," the boy said. "I have never been saved."

"Son, I want to tell you how to be saved," continued the pastor. "I want to tell you how to die. I want to tell you how to meet God." The pastor read to him those simple passages that we have just quoted on how to be saved. The boy broke in, and looking into the face of the pastor in astonishment, said, "Is it that easy?"

The pastor replied: "Son, it is easy for you, but not for him. You see, he took our sins and bore them in his own body on the tree. He suffered in our stead. By his stripes we are healed."

Salvation is easy for us, because he won that battle for us. He took our sins for us. He paid the penalty for us. He died for us that we might never die but have everlasting life in him. How to be saved is simply trusting Jesus. "And he preached unto him Jesus."

The Act of Conversion Is the Committal of Your Life to Jesus

Third, the mighty act of conversion is always a simple act, committing your life to the Lord Jesus.

One time I got on my knees and said: "Dear God, you say in your Word, 'Believe on the Lord Jesus Christ, and thou shalt be saved.' What is it to believe? What is saving faith? What is saving trust?" The Lord spoke to my heart with this passage in 2 Timothy: "For I know whom I have believed, and am persuaded that he is able to keep that which I have committed unto him against that day" (1:12). What is it to trust in Jesus? It is that simple act of committing your life to the Savior. "This day, this evening, tomorrow, and forever I do commit my life to Thee, I place it in Thy dear nail-pierced hands." The great act of conversion is the committal of your life to the Lord Jesus. From now on my life belongs to him— my heart, my destiny, my every tomorrow.

In the days of the missionary preaching to the Blanket Indians and to the Plains Indians, there was a preacher who had a tent and had pitched it in Western Oklahoma on the high plains. He was preaching the gospel to a Blanket Indian tribe. As the meeting progressed and as he was preaching the gospel to those Indians, in one of his services the Indian chief came down and stood in front of the missionary. Looking up into his face, he said, "Missionary, Indian chief give his tomahawk to Jesus," and he laid it at the missionary's feet. The missionary paid no attention to him but just kept on preaching about Jesus.

The Indian chief arose a second time, walked down to the front, and said, "Missionary, Indian chief give his blanket to Jesus," and he laid his blanket at the feet of the missionary. The missionary paid no attention to him at all, but just kept on preaching about the Lord Jesus.

He arose again, went outside of the tent, tied his pony to a stake of the tent, walked back, and looked at the missionary and said, "Missionary, Indian chief give his pony to Jesus." That was the last possession that he had. The missionary paid no attention to him at all but just kept on preaching to him about Jesus.

The chief arose one other time, came down to the front. This time he knelt in front of the preacher, and looking up to his face said, "Missionary, Indian chief give himself to Jesus."

That is what it is to be saved. We do not buy or bribe our way into the kingdom of heaven. We just give ourselves in faith, in trust, and in committal to the Lord Jesus, and he saves us. He writes our name in the Lamb's Book of Life. He numbers us among God's redeemed. The great act of conversion is the committal of your life to Jesus. "And he preached unto him Jesus."

Entrance into the Church Is Through Obedience
to the Commandment of Jesus

Will you notice that the entrance into the church of
the family of God is in obedience to the great commandment, the Great Commission of the Lord Jesus. We are
to go and to make disciples of all of the people, baptizing
them in the name of the Father, of the Son, and of the
Holy Spirit. In 1 Corinthians 12 we read: "For by one
Spirit are we all baptized into one body" (v. 13).

There are two kinds of baptism. There is the Spirit
baptism, when God adds us to the body of the Lord
and we become a member of the household of faith. It
is a baptismal work of the Holy Spirit. There is also a
baptism in water. The outward sign of salvation is water
baptism when we are baptized into the body, the family
of Christ. Our text says:

> As they went on their way, they came unto a
> certain water: and the eunuch said, See, here is water;
> what doth hinder me to be baptized?
>
> And Philip said, If thou believest with all thine
> heart, thou mayest. And he answered and said, I
> believe that Jesus Christ is the Son of God.
>
> And he commanded the chariot to stand still: and
> they went down both into the water, both Philip
> and the eunuch; and he baptized him.
>
> And when they were come up out of the water,
> the Spirit of the Lord caught away Philip, that the
> eunuch saw him no more: and he went on his way
> rejoicing (Acts 8:36–39).

Our entrance into the church, into the body of Christ,
is in our baptism, a simple, humble obedience to the

Great Commission and the great commandment of Jesus.
That is the first thing that will come into the heart of
someone who trusts in the Lord as Savior. "Pastor, I want
to be baptized just as Jesus was, just as he commanded,
and just as all of the saved of God have been baptized
in the New Testament."

Our Assignment Is Praising Jesus

Look at the text: "And he went on his way rejoicing."
Our assignment now and forever is praising the blessed
Lord Jesus. He is everything; he is all in all. We are to
love him, serve him, dedicate heart, life, and tomorrow
to him. Is not that the sign, the image, and the revelation
of heaven itself? "Unto him who loved us, and washed
us from our sins in his own blood . . . to him be glory
and dominion for ever and ever" (Rev. 1:5–6). This is
the paean of praise that is the text of the anthem that
we shall sing in heaven and in earth, just praising Jesus,
our all in all.

> I entered once a home of care,
> And penury and want were there,
>   But joy and peace withal.
> I asked the aged mother whence
> Her helpless widowhood's defense;
>   She answered, "Christ is all."

> I saw the martyr at the stake,
> The flames could not his courage shake,
>   Nor death his soul apall.
> I asked him whence his strength was given,
> He looked triumphantly to heaven
>   And answered, "Christ is all."

I stood beside the dying bed,
Where lay a child with aching head,
    Waiting Jesus' call.
I saw him smile, t'was sweet as May,
And as his spirit passed away,
    He whispered, "Christ is all."

I dreamed that hoary time had fled,
The earth and sea gave up their dead,
    A fire dissolved this ball.
I saw the church's ransomed throng,
I caught the burden of their song,
    T'was this, that Christ was all in all.

A people waiting for the Lord, loving the Lord, serving
the Lord, committing heart and life to the blessed Jesus
we are to be. "And he preached unto him Jesus." Only
Jesus. Jesus only.

4.
Knocking at the Door

Behold, I stand at the door, and knock: if any man hear my voice, and open the door, I will come in to him, and will sup with him, and he with me (Rev. 3:20).

In St. Paul's Cathedral, London, is displayed one of the most famous pictures of Jesus ever placed on canvas. It is Holman Hunt's picture entitled, *The Light of the World*. In the painting the figure of our Lord is standing before a door and he is knocking, seeking entrance. That is an everlasting and eternal picture of our living Lord, knocking at the door, and it is a picture of the whole Christian revelation of God from the beginning to the end. It is a picture of our Lord Father, the great and mighty God Jehovah, visiting his people.

In Genesis 3 there is told the story of Adam and Eve, who, even after they had fallen and had hidden themselves among the trees of the garden, hear the voice of the Lord God as he was walking in the garden in the cool of the day. The Lord asks, "Adam, where art thou?" He is a seeking and a searching God from the beginning, knocking at the door.

The first chapter of the book of Ruth, begins a story so sad and traumatic for Naomi, who has lost by death her husband and her two sons in the land of Moab. After the sorrow of those days, she turns her face back to Bethlehem in Judah, for Naomi says, "I have heard that the

Lord has visited his people in giving them bread."

In the eighth Psalm is this beautiful song of praise to Almighty God: "When I consider thy heavens, the work of thy fingers, the moon and the stars, which thou hast ordained; What is man, that thou art mindful of him? and the son of man, that thou visitest him?" (vv. 3–4). He is a visiting God knocking at the door.

All of the prophecies present a picture, an outline, of the coming Messiah and Savior of the world. He is always pictured as visiting his people. In Zechariah 9, for example, we read:

> Rejoice greatly, O daughter of Zion; shout, O daughter of Jerusalem: behold, thy King cometh unto thee: he is just, and having salvation; lowly . . . and he shall speak peace unto the heathen: and his dominion shall be from sea even to sea, and from the ends of the earth (vv. 9–10).

Coming, visiting, knocking at the door. Isaiah said, "His name will be called *Emanu-El*, 'God is with us.' "

Christ's Way

That is a picture also of the life and ministry of our Lord in the days of his flesh, visiting the people, knocking at the door. He is what is called a peripatetic teacher. He taught as he walked and visited among the people. From village to village, from town to town, and from house to house did the Lord carry the message of Christ, of salvation, knocking at the door. He even went to one certain town where there was a certain tree, and in that certain tree there was a certain sinner, and the Lord called that certain sinner by his name and said, "Today at a certain hour I will eat dinner in your house." That is the Lord Jesus. When the people said, "He has gone to be the guest of a man who is a sinner," the Lord justified his ministry and what he had done with this wonderful sentence, "For the Son of man is come to seek and to save that which was lost" (Luke 19:10). The ministry of our Lord—knocking at the door.

The Way Jesus Taught His Disciples

That is the way he taught his disciples, and that is the way he teaches us. Look at the difference between us and him. We say: "Let us stand on the edge of the field and let us lift up our voice and call, 'All of the acres out there in the field, come up and get sown.' " That is what we say. But the Lord said it like this: "A sower went forth to sow in the field."

We stand on the shore and say, "All you fishes out there, come up here and get caught." But Jesus said, "Launch out into the deep, and let down the net for a draft."

On the edge of the wilderness, we build a great monument with a spire, maybe with stained-glass windows and with comfortable pews. We put a sign on the outside of the mausoleum and say, "All of you lost sheep, if you happen to wander by, come in and get saved." That is the way we do. But the Lord taught us, "The shepherd left his ninety and nine and went out in the wilderness to seek until he found the lost sheep." What a difference!

In Luke 14 the Lord sent the disciples out into the streets and lanes of the city, into the byways and highways, to compel the people to come in. That is the teaching and the training of the Lord. In Matthew 10 the Lord called his twelve apostles and sent them out to knock at the doors of the homes. In Luke 10 the Lord called the other seventy also and sent them out to visit in the homes and the villages of the people. That is the Lord. All of the Gospels climax in what we call the Great Commission. The commission is simply one little word, *Go.* Go into all the world. Go and make disciples of all the people. Going, they taught and they preached the Lord Jesus.

The Apostles and Preachers of Christ
Follow His Example

Now I want us to see how the disciples faithfully followed through in that teaching and beautiful example of the Lord, visiting and knocking at the door. Acts 5 closes like this: "Daily in the temple, and in every house, they ceased not to teach and preach Jesus Christ" (Acts 5:42)—knocking at the door.

Acts 8 begins: "They were all scattered abroad throughout the regions of Judaea and Samaria. . . . Therefore they that were scattered abroad went every where preaching the word" (Acts 8:1,4).

There is a marvelous illustration of the incarnation and implementation of that method of the Lord in the ministry of the apostle Paul at Ephesus. I would suppose that in Ephesus that is one of the greatest outpourings of the Spirit of the Lord. The effectiveness of the preaching of the gospel in Paul's missionary visit to the queenly city of Ephesus was phenomenal. He turned the whole province to the Lord Jesus. It was in that ministry that the seven churches of Asia were founded, a vast and startling conversion. So we ask, "How did Paul do that?"

I know what you are going to say, because it is what everyone says. Paul did that because he was a powerful and mighty preacher of the gospel. All my life have I heard men stand up in vast conventions and convocations and say of a preacher, "He is the greatest preacher since the apostle Paul." I know what they mean by that, and you do too. When he says, "This man is the greatest preacher since the apostle Paul," the announcer means that the one he is introducing possesses a majestic presence, that he stands with a sweeping personality, and he rises from one peroration to another in stentorian tones and oratorical flights.

It would do us good once in awhile to read the Bible. Just exactly what kind of preacher was Paul and what did he look like? In 2 Corinthians 10:10 Paul says, "Say they . . . his bodily presence is weak, and his speech contemptible." That is what people said about Paul when they heard him preach.

How did Paul do such a vast and tremendous work as he did in the great city of Ephesus? Here again one should read the Bible. Paul called the Ephesian elders down to Miletus on the seaside, and he described to them his three-year ministry in the city of Ephesus. He said: "Watch, and remember, that by the space of three years I ceased not to warn every one night and day with tears" (Acts 20:31). Paul did his work from house to house, testifying both to the Jews and to the Greeks; that is, to everybody in the row, everybody who lived on the street, testifying repentance toward God and faith toward our Lord Jesus Christ (vv. 20–21).

I submit to you that any preacher in the world and any church family can do that, and the same blessing that fell upon Paul in Ephesus will fall upon the church or the preacher who will do that simple thing, of testifying repentance toward God and faith toward our Lord Jesus Christ from house to house.

When I was in school, I had a little church where I preached once a month. While I was preaching at my little church, a committee of men from another commu-

nity came to me and said: "Our church is closed, and
the door is nailed fast and shut. But we have many young
people in our community. Would you come over on a
Sunday afternoon and preach for us?" I said, yes. So I
went over to that little country church.

We removed the nails and opened the door. We swept
out the church house. We replaced panes of glass which
had been broken out. We cut down the weeds that had
grown up to the eaves of the church. Do you know what
I did? At the first road that started by that little church,
I walked down the road and knocked at every door of
every house fronting the road. When the people came
to the door, I said: "I am the pastor of a little church
down the road. Are you Christian people?" If they said,
"Yes, we are Christians here," I said, "May I come in
and read to you out of God's blessed Word, and may I
kneel with you in prayer?" I would go and read to them
out of the Bible and kneel with them in prayer. If I came
to a house where they were not Christians, and knocked
at the door I would ask: "May I come in and tell you
about the blessed Savior and pray with you, that you
might know God?" I would go in the house, talk to them
about Jesus, and pray for their souls that they might
be saved.

You already know what happened. One could not get
into the church. People filled the church and the church
yard. They looked in through the windows and the doors.
When I concluded the revival meeting that summer, we
had the largest baptismal service that county had ever
seen. Throngs of people stood on the riverbank watching
as I baptized those scores of converts.

Anybody can do that. That is God's way. That is the
way the Lord blesses. Not our brilliant expositions, not
our stentorian voices and our magnificent gestures, but

God blesses that seeking heart and interceding spirit knocking at the door.

The Christian Way

May I point out that this visiting, this knocking at the door, this bringing the message of Christ face to face, heart to heart, home to home, and house to house is at the very soul and center of the Christian faith? The pastor of the church at Jerusalem, the Lord's brother, James, said: "Pure religion and undefiled before God and the Father is this, To visit . . ." (Jas. 1:27). Pure religion is to visit, to knock at the door.

I know how we are, and we are all alike. You and I go to a tremendous convocation, and we stand among the thousands and thousands of people in a vast auditorium rising tier upon tier. When we look at the vast gathering, we say, "This is the faith!" Strange, the Lord never mentioned it; he never referred to it. We go to a marvelous mausoleum, a glorious edifice, a vast ecclesiastical structure, and look at a beautiful and pompous service. When it is done, we go out the door and we say, "This is the faith!" Strange, the Lord never mentioned it; he never referred to it. We go to a service and there is an eloquent preacher who stands up and delivers a message, rising from one oratorical peroration to another, and when the sermon is done, we say, "Man, that is the faith!" Jesus never referred to it; he never mentioned it.

Do you know what the Lord did say? He did have something to say about a cup of cold water given in the name of a disciple. He did have something to say about seeking the one lost sheep until he found it, searching for the one lost coin until it is recovered, praying for the one prodigal boy until he comes home. That is

the Lord, knocking at the door. "Pure religion and undefiled before the heavenly Father is this, to knock at the
door."

There was a Sunday School teacher who had a pupil
named Mary who was absent one Sunday. The teacher
wrote a card, saying: "Dear Mary, we missed you at Sunday School. Be sure to be present next Sunday." Two
weeks passed and little Mary was not present. So the
Sunday School teacher wrote another card to Mary; "We
missed you last Sunday. Be sure to come to Sunday
School next Sunday." The teacher waited another two
weeks. Mary again was not present, so the teacher wrote;
"Dear Mary, we have missed you in Sunday School. We
want you to be present next Sunday." The teacher, coming from the post office, happened to meet the mother
of the little girl. The Sunday School teacher, so proud
of herself, said: "Oh, I am so happy to see you. I have
just been to the post office, and for the fourth time I
have mailed a card to your little girl telling her how
much we missed her in Sunday School." The mother
sadly replied: "You do not need to write any more cards.
After a long illness, yesterday we buried our little girl,
Mary." It may be good religion to write a card. It may
be acceptable to mail a letter. But pure religion and undefiled before God is this: "I have come to see you in the
name of Jesus. We missed little Mary" or, "We miss you,"
or "Are you Christians?" or "Do you know the Lord?"
or "Have you been saved?"

As long as that picture of Jesus stands in the Bible
knocking at the door, just so long will real religion, pure
and undefiled, be defined by our sharing the faith house
to house, from heart to heart, from people to people.
That is the faith. Then when we gather in the sanctuary,
have the services, listen to the expounding of the Word

of God, and we stand and sing our hymns of appeal, then we rejoice to see the people coming down the aisle whom we have invited to the Lord. We know them by name. We have seen them; we have talked to them. We have visited with them, and we have told them about the Lord Jesus. When they come, they are not strangers; they are friends for whom Jesus died and for whom we have prayed.

Grant it, Lord, that our church services are just sounding boards where people come together to rejoice in the salvation of our mighty and marvelous Lord!

5.
Saul, the New Christian

And there was a certain disciple at Damascus, named Ananias; and to him said the Lord in a vision, Ananias. And he said, Behold, I am here, Lord.

And the Lord said unto him, Arise, and go into the street which is called Straight, and enquire in the house of Judas for one called Saul, of Tarsus: for, behold, he prayeth,

And hath seen in a vision a man named Ananias coming in, and putting his hand on him, that he might receive his sight.

Then Ananias answered, Lord, I have heard by many of this man, how much evil he hath done to thy saints at Jerusalem:

And here he hath authority from the chief priests to bind all that call on thy name.

But the Lord said unto him, Go thy way: for he is a chosen vessel unto me, to bear my name before the Gentiles, and kings, and the children of Israel:

For I will shew him how great things he must suffer for my name's sake.

And Ananias went his way, and entered into the house; and putting his hands on him said, Brother Saul, the Lord, even Jesus, that appeared unto thee in the way as thou camest, hath sent me, that thou mightest receive thy sight, and be filled with the Holy Ghost.

And immediately there fell from his eyes as it had been scales: and he received sight forthwith, and arose, and was baptized.

And when he had received meat, he was strengthened. Then was Saul certain days with the disciples which were at Damascus.

*And straightway he preached Christ in the synagogues, that he
is the Son of God.*

*But all that heard him were amazed, and said; Is not this he
that destroyed them which called on this name in Jerusalem, and
came hither for that intent, that he might bring them bound unto
the chief priests?*

*But Saul increased the more in strength, and confounded the Jews
which dwelt at Damascus, proving that this is very Christ (Acts
9:10–22).*

Acts 9 records the greatest triumph in the history of
Christianity, a master miracle—the conversion of Saul
of Tarsus. There are two tremendous pillars upon which
rest the authenticity and authority of the Christian faith.
They are like the columns that Solomon built in front
of the beautiful Temple in Jerusalem. One he called Boaz,
and the other he called Jachin. One he called "strength,"
and one he called "glory and beauty." There are two
great columns upon which the Christian faith rests. One
is the resurrection of Jesus Christ, and the other is the
conversion of the apostle Paul. If either one of those
columns falls to the ground, the very fabric of the Christian faith is unraveled.

Out of all of the men one could name, there has never
been a more unlikely prospect for conversion than this
brilliant, gifted, dedicated, and zealous young rabbi. Saul
of Tarsus was born of a long and honorable parentage
and pedigree in the Jewish race. He was a student in
the school of Gamaliel, one of the seven great rabbans
of the Talmud. He was almost without peer in his brilliant
scholasticism and in his grasp of godly, heavenly revelation. He was shrewder than Judas Iscariot. He was more
ardent than Simon Peter. He was a volcano of a man.

That Saul of Tarsus should be converted is like converting an army with banners. It is like converting a nation, a world.

The Apt Scholar in Terror

Saul was an apt student in terror and persecution. For example, he is introduced to us at the first in Acts 7: "The witnesses laid down their clothes at a young man's feet, whose name was Saul. And they stoned Stephen . . ." (vv. 58–59).

Then we find in Acts 8:1 that "Saul was consenting unto his death." In the third verse we read, "As for Saul, he made havock of the church, entering into every house, and haling men and women committed them to prison." Continuing in Acts, we read in the ninth chapter:

> And Saul, yet breathing out threatenings and slaughter against the disciples of the Lord, went unto the high priest,
> And desired of him letters to Damascus to the synagogues, that if he found any of this way, whether they were men or women, he might bring them bound unto Jerusalem (vv. 1–2).

Saul grew in his fury. At first he was just presiding over the death of Stephen, finding himself filled with pleasure and gladness over the execution of that godly deacon and servant of Jesus. Then taking a two-fisted hold on the entire persecuting, terrorizing assignment (men, women, and children were alike to Saul), he beat them, forced them to blaspheme, saw the blood run down their backs, and finally he committed them to prison and to death. It is a strange thing about human nature. The taste of blood is not a natural taste, but it feeds on itself, and the man who finds himself in a complex of terror, persecution, murder, and blood will find himself increasingly involved in it. So it was with Saul of Tarsus, beginning in Jerusalem, and then persecuting unto strange cities. He thrived in terrorism and bloodshed.

Saul's Meeting with Jesus

Saul's meeting Jesus in the way was of all things a heavenly intervention. Saul, on his way to Damascus, was much persuaded that Jesus was a dead man and rightfully dead. Jesus had been executed under Pontius Pilate between two malefactors, two thieves, two traitors, two insurrectionists, two murderers, and he deserved to be executed between those two felons. He was a blasphemer, this Nazarene. Saul of Tarsus had said: "We know that God spoke to Moses, but as for this heretic Jesus, he was a deceiver and he led people astray and he deserved to die. Having been crucified, he is a dead man." That was Saul of Tarsus.

Then in his fury and rage, as he journeyed to Damascus, there standing in the way is *that* dead man—glorified, immortalized, and brilliant—above the shining of the sun. He stood before Saul and asks, "Saul, Saul, why persecutest thou me?" Saul replies in Acts 9:4: "Lord, I never persecuted you. I never cast thee in prison. I never beat thee or stoned thee. I never lifted my voice or my hand against thee. Who art thou, Lord?" The Lord replied, "I am Jesus, that dead man, that executed malefactor and felon who died between two thieves. I am Jesus of Nazareth whom thou persecutest."

What a remarkable identification! The Lord is one with his people. When they cast stones upon Stephen, the Lord said: "Those stones crushed me. When you haled them into prison, these humblest disciples of the Lord, you imprisoned me. When you beat them till the blood ran down their backs, it was my blood that fell to the ground. When you put them to death, you were slaying me. When they suffered and cried, I suffered and cried. Their tears are my tears, their sorrow is my sorrow."

Christ identifies himself with his people. He still does. He is one with us and we are one with him. And now behold this penitent Saul of Tarsus!

The Humble Penitent

Did you ever see a man change as that man changed? The Bible says: "When his eyes were opened, he saw no man; but they led him by the hand, and brought him into Damascus." Ah, can you believe such an event? One would have thought that he would enter Damascus like a conqueror, like a storm, or like a victorious general. Instead, Saul is being led into the city like a blind beggar. One would have thought Saul would have entered the city in victory with letters of commendation from the chief priest in Jerusalem. Instead, he entered like a poverty-stricken cripple. They led him by the hand into Damascus. The distance from Jerusalem into Damascus is 136 miles, and the journey was six days long. Before this encounter with the Lord Jesus, Saul of Tarsus would have urged his company on, his nostrils dilated with indignation and his eyes flaming with a fire of anger, haling these humble believers in Jesus to prison, to incarceration, to beating, and to death; but now, entering the city of Jerusalem, Saul has to be led by the hand. The Lord said to Ananias of Saul, "behold, he prayeth" (Acts 9:11). The lion is lying down with the lamb. What an unbelievable miracle!

An old poet said to a young seaman:

Aboard a man-o'-war, son,
There is just one choice,
Duty or mutiny.

So it is when a man meets Christ. It is either, "Lord, what wilt Thou have me to do?" or it is a rejection of the will of God for your life. This Saul of Tarsus, meeting with the Lord in the way, bowed before him and said, "Lord, what wilt thou have me to do?"

The Preacher and Pleader

Now we are introduced to Saul, Paul, the preacher, and the pleader. "And straightway he preached Christ in the synagogues, that he is the Son of God" (Acts 9:20). Look at the turn in that man's life. What an amazing, miraculous thing has happened! Saul had been a persecutor and now he is a Christian. Look at the change in his life. He had been a terrible wolf ravaging the flock. Now what does he do? Does he turn to imprison Jews? Does he turn to waste Pharisees and Sadducees? In terror does he ravage the people to whom he had belonged? No. In his turn he does not say, "Now I am on their side, and what I used to do to them I am now going to do to you." No. When he turns and stands with the scroll of the Holy Scriptures in his hand, he reasons and he pleads and he preaches and he calls men to repentance and to faith in the blessed Lord Jesus our Savior.

How different from the way unbelief always works! "What do you do?" says the man of the world, the man outside of Christ. "What do you do with these heretics and these enemies?" "This is what you do," he says. "You stab them, you stone them, you imprison them, you burn them, you drown them, and you kill them." But what does the Christian do? His sword is now the sword of the Spirit. His chains are now the chains that bind him to the intercessory altars of God. His stones and his iron bars are those that he builds cemented with the love of Jesus and encompassing those who find strength and refuge in him.

What an amazing change! Saul was stoned. Did he rise from that stoning in Lystra to cast stones back to those heathen Greeks who dragged him out for dead? No. He did not stone anymore. He was imprisoned in Philippi, having been liberated in Christ. Does he seek to imprison those who imprisoned him? No. He is praying for those who mistreated him. His sufferings are named in 2 Corinthians 11. His reply is one of intercession and glory in his sufferings. "Therefore," he is saying, "I take pleasure in reproaches, in persecutions, in stripes, and in imprisonments, for when I am weak, then am I strong." It is another day. It is another way. It is another message. It is a new gospel!

The Moral, Spiritual Appeal of the Christian Faith

Now let me speak of our Christian faith. As the faith developed and as the story of the church continued, when one turns to the pages of history, he will find them stained with blood by the Inquisition and by the persecutions of the church. They exchanged solicitude for the sword. They propagated the faith with the fire, the flame, and the faggot. They enforced doctrine with the gloom of the dungeon. Is that Christian? Is that the spirit of Jesus? Never. The spirit of the Christian is always one of intercession, of pleading, of prayer, of reason, of persuasion. The preacher is always like the *parakletos,* the Paraclete, the Holy Spirit, pleading with the man to give his heart and his life to Jesus. "This is the way, walk ye in it."

Our reply to the world is always one of grace, love,

and intercession, just as the apostle Paul turned from his life of bitterness and persecution to give himself in love for his brethren, his people. He said, "I could wish that myself were accursed from Christ for my brethren, my kinsmen according to the flesh." Then he said, "My heart's desire and prayer to God for Israel is, that they might be saved." This is the response of the Christian to the world.

As my predecessor, the great George W. Truett, once said before a vast congregation, "If I could lift my little finger to force you to be a Christian, I would not lift the weight of my little finger, for the soul is free." The heart of God made the human soul to be free to make its own decision, its own volitional choice. I am absolutely free before God. I can choose for him. I can choose against him. I can crown or crucify Jesus, but it has to be out of the fullness of my heart that I decide. The assignment of the preacher is to be a pleader, an inviter, an encourager, and a reasoner. Come for Jesus' sake, come. Eternal life is ours for the having, for the taking.

6.

That They Might Be Saved

Brethren, my heart's desire and prayer to God for Israel is, that they might be saved.

For I bear them record that they have a zeal of God, but not according to knowledge.

For they being ignorant of God's righteousness, and going about to establish their own righteousness, have not submitted themselves unto the righteousness of God.

For Christ is the end of the law for righteousness to every one that believeth.

For Moses describeth the righteousness which is of the law, That the man which doeth those things shall live by them.

But the righteousness which is of faith speaketh on this wise, Say not in thine heart, Who shall ascend into heaven? (that is, to bring Christ down from above:)

Or, Who shall descend into the deep? (that is, to bring up Christ again from the dead.)

But what saith it? The word is nigh thee, even in thy mouth, and in thy heart: that is, the word of faith, which we preach;

That if thou shalt confess with thy mouth the Lord Jesus, and shalt believe in thine heart that God hath raised him from the dead, thou shalt be saved.

For with the heart man believeth unto righteousness; and with the mouth confession is made unto salvation.

For the scripture saith, Whosoever believeth on him shall not be ashamed.

For there is no difference between the Jew and the Greek: for the same Lord over all is rich unto all that call upon him.

For whosoever shall call upon the name of the Lord shall be saved (Rom. 10:1–13).

Our text presents an astonishing avowal which is addressed to the Gentiles, not to the Jewish people. The church at Rome was a Gentile church, and the apostle Paul was appointed of God as a messenger to the Gentiles. All of his ministry he was involved in preaching the gospel of Christ to the Roman world, to the Gentile world. Therefore it makes the meaning of the text all the more poignant when we read, "Brethren, my heart's desire and prayer to God for Israel is, that they might be saved" (Rom. 10:1). Paul began Romans 9 with the same earnest intercession:

> I say the truth in Christ, I lie not, my conscience also bearing me witness in the Holy Ghost,
>
> That I have great heaviness and continual sorrow in my heart.
>
> For I could wish that myself were accursed from Christ for my brethren, my kinsmen according to the flesh (vv. 1–3).

What he actually says is: "For I could wish that myself were damned in hell for my brethren, for my kinsmen, according to the flesh. Brethren, my heart's desire and prayer to God for my people is that they might be saved." This is the apostle to the Gentiles saying these words in behalf of his own family, of his own people, and of his own nation.

The passage is altogether explicable and pardonable, for however a man may be interested in the salvation of those who are across the seas, people of other languages, tongues, colors, and nations, our first and primary interest is in those who belong to our own families, who live in our own city, who breathe the same air that we breathe and who live on our same streets. Our heart's desire and prayer to God, our first care, our first interest, and our first love is that you might be saved. What a tragedy if we gave the energies of our lives for the conversion of the lost in other continents, in other nations, among other peoples; and then our own people, our own families, and our own loved ones were lost! "Brethren, my heart's desire and prayer to God for my own people is that they might be saved."

There is no one who can lift us up as you can, you who belong to our own families. The reverse is also no less true. There is no one who can bow us down in brokenheartedness and in unspeakable sorrow and tears as you can. However the world may be outside and beyond us, our first love, care, and prayer is always for you.

The Reason They Were Lost

Why were they lost? This is the purpose of Paul's writing. He says that some of them are lost because they say the way to be saved is up. Men must ascend into heaven and find the way of salvation. They avow that the way to be saved is like climbing a ladder, rung after rung. If I can be better and better and better, and if I can be still better and better, and if I can go upward and upward on a ladder that leans against the bulwarks and the parapets of heaven, if I can just climb high enough, then I can finally be saved (Rom. 10:6).

There are others who say just the opposite. They say that the way to be saved is not something that a man can just plainly see or do, but the way to be saved is to dig and to dig and to dig, and to study, to study,

and to study, ferreting out the truth of God. Finally, if
we can study long enough, dig deep enough, and go down
to the depths enough, then we can bring up the way
to God and how to be saved (v. 2).

The apostle Paul, in discussing those two ideas, says,
"What saith the Word of God? What does God say about
being saved?" Then he quotes, "The word is nigh thee,
even in thy mouth, and in thy heart: that is, the word
of faith, which we preach." The way to be saved is nearer
than the breath you breathe, and it is nearer than our
hands and our feet. Salvation is that close. It is that near,
namely:

> That if thou shalt confess with thy mouth the
> Lord Jesus, and shalt believe in thine heart that God
> hath raised him from the dead, thou shalt be saved.
> For with the heart man believeth unto righteous-
> ness; and with the mouth confession is made unto
> salvation (vv. 9–10).

That is the way, God says, we are to be saved. We
are to believe on Jesus in our hearts, and we are to openly,
publicly, and unashamedly, before men and angels, confess him with our mouths. That is the one way of salvation. That is the way of salvation for the richest man
who ever lived. That is the way of salvation for the poor-
est man who ever lived. That is the way of salvation
for the oldest man who ever lived. That is the way of
salvation for the youngest lad who ever came into the
kingdom of God. That is the way of salvation for the
learned student and academician in the highest university. It is also the way of salvation for the unlettered,
untaught man who has never learned even how to read.

All of us are saved alike. There is just one way, and it is as close as our hands and feet, as the very breath that we breathe.

I have a friend who is now retired, a brilliant man. I asked him one day, "How many books have you written?" At that time he had written more than fifty-five, a veritable library. He is one of the most learned men that I ever knew, capable and dedicated to the Lord. One time we were preaching through an evangelistic conference together, and after the service, we were talking about the days gone by and our assignments now. I turned to him and said, "Would you tell me how you were saved, when you were saved, and how it came about?"

He answered me, never referring to a Hebrew word, though he is adept in the original language of the Old Testament. He did not refer to a Greek word, root, or participle, though he can use the Greek language as well as we use English. He did not refer to the vast erudition that has characterized his life for the years since his graduation from the seminary. Do you know what he said?

He said: "When I was a little boy I felt the burden of my heart that I wanted to accept Christ as my Savior. At a service in the church when the preacher had preached his sermon, the people stood and sang an invitation hymn:

> If you are tired of the load of your sin,
> Let Jesus come into your heart;
> If you desire a new life to begin,
> Let Jesus come into your heart.
>
> Just now, your doubtings give o'er;
> Just now, reject him no more;

Just now, throw open the door;
Let Jesus come into your heart.

Leila N. Morris

He said, "That day I accepted Jesus into my heart and
I was saved."

Is not that right? However the man be in life, rich or
poor, learned or unlearned, old or young, we are all saved
alike by trusting Jesus in our hearts.

Did you ever think of the ark, big as it was, holding
all of the species of the animals that were to propagate
and proliferate in the earth? Did you ever think that
the ark had only one door? There is just one door; there
is just one way to be saved. Through one door of the
great ark, the giant elephant lumbered in and the little
snail crawled in. Into that one door went the great eagle
as he swooped out of the blue of the sky, and into that
one door hopped the little wren. Into that one door went
Noah and his wife; Shem, Ham, and Japheth, their three
boys, and their wives. They were all saved alike. That
is a type and a picture of our salvation. All of us are
saved alike. We go through that one door of the Lord
Jesus.

One of the most moving services for me that I ever
conducted was in the church at Muskogee, Oklahoma.
Sunday morning when I had finished preaching and was
pressing the invitation, down the aisle came a little boy
named Jimmy Marlin. He was ten years of age. He came
to me and said, "Today I want to take Jesus as my Savior,
and I want to be baptized." So little Jimmy Marlin sat
down on the front pew.

Then I lifted up my face and down the aisle was coming
Mickey McFarland who was seventy-four years of age

and the most famous outlaw in Indian Territory days. He came down the aisle and he took my hand saying, "Sir, today I want to take Jesus as my Savior, and I want to be baptized and belong to the church." He was seated by the little boy.

I lifted up my face and down the aisle came old Bird Doublehead, a full-blooded Cherokee Indian who was one hundred and three years of age. He came tottering down the aisle to me. Taking my hand, he said, "I want to take Jesus as my Savior, and I want to be baptized and be a member of the church."

There they sat together, the little ten-year-old boy, Jimmy Marlin, and by his side, Mickey McFarland, a famous Indian outlaw from Territory days, then by his side old Bird Doublehead, a full-blooded Cherokee Indian, one hundred and three years of age. All three of them were saved alike. The little boy, the hardened outlaw, and the aged Indian said, "I want to take Jesus as my Savior." That says it, and that does it. Christ honors each one's act of faith. They were baptized into the fellowship of the precious body of Christ, the kingdom of our Lord, in that dear church. There is only one way to be saved, and that is a simple way, as simple as God could make it.

The Triumphant, Climactic Word

Look at the climactic verse in the passage: "For whosoever shall call upon the name of the Lord shall be saved" (Rom. 10:13). That means anybody. The whole Bible ends with the same invitation. We read in Revelation 22:7: "And the Spirit and the bride say, Come. And let him that heareth say, Come. And let him that is athirst come. And whosoever will, let him take the water of life freely."

My brethren, I may admire the Lord and be lost. I

may sing about the Lord and be lost. I may write books about the Lord and be lost. I may know and be an authority intellectually about the Lord and be lost. In fact, I could even preach about the Lord and be lost. But one thing I cannot do. I cannot call upon his name and be lost, for if I call upon his name, I will be saved. God will do something to my heart and to my life.

In our church there was a blessed young mother who had a little boy. She came to church so faithfully bringing her son, but her husband never came or showed any interest. She came to me and said, "Oh, that my husband would be a Christian; that he would come to church with my little boy and me; that he would be saved; that we could have a happy Christian home!"

I said, "We will pray, and I will try to win your husband to the Lord." I tried many times. He drank; he was uninterested; he was worldly; and he made no response at all. The days passed, and she disappeared. She did not come to church anymore, and I did not see the little boy anymore. So I made inquiry and found that the couple had broken up their home, they were getting a divorce, and she was working at a place of employment. I went down to the place where she was working and said, "I have heard that you have broken up your home and that you are getting a divorce."

She said, "Yes, it is just impossible that we could live together with his drinking and all of the things that go with it; so we are getting a divorce. I have sent my little boy to my parents' house for him to be raised, and I have a job."

I said, "Why do you not come to church?"

She said: "There was never a divorce in our family, and I am so heartbroken and ashamed. That is why I do not come to church."

On a Sunday morning while I was standing in the pulpit reading the text and getting ready to preach, I saw her husband come in the back door and sit down on the back pew. After the service was over and all the people had left, he tarried and came down to the front to me. He said, "I have ruined my life; I have ruined my home; and I have broken my wife's heart. O God, that I could be saved!"

I said, "Sir, you sit down here by my side." I took the Bible and read to him how a man can be saved. One of the passages that I read is the one in our text: "If thou shalt confess with thy mouth the Lord Jesus, and believe in thine heart that God hath raised him from the dead, thou shalt be saved." Then I said, "Get down here on your knees by my side." I put my arm around him and prayed for his soul.

After I had prayed just for a few minutes, he put his hand on me and said, "Pastor, wait just a minute. Something has happened to my heart. I have been changed! I have been saved!"

I said, "Let us tell God about it." So he told Jesus, thanked him for saving him, for forgiving his sins, and for giving him a new heart and a new life. I praised God with him. That Sunday night when I gave the invitation, down the aisle he came, and I baptized him at the close of the service.

I waited about two days and then I went to a certain address and knocked at the door. His wife came to the door and said, "I know why you are here."

"Then you have heard?" I asked.

"Yes," she said. "Come in."

I went in and sat down by her side.

She said, "Last night there was a knock at the door. I went to the door and there stood my husband. For the first time in my life I saw him with a Bible in his hand. He said, 'Dear wife, may I come in?' "

She invited him in.

She continued: "He sat there in the chair where you are now seated and opened the Bible and said: 'Sweetheart, I have found the Lord; I have been saved; God has forgiven me my sins. May I read to you out of the Bible?' He read a passage out of God's Word. Then he said, 'Sweetheart, would you kneel by my side and let us pray?' Down there on our knees we put our home together again. God forgave us our sins. Today I have sent word for my little boy to come home."

The following Sunday morning when I stood up in the pulpit to preach, there was that man, the mother, and between them, their son.

"For whosoever shall call on the name of the Lord shall be saved." God said that. God's Spirit is in that. When I ask Jesus to help me, he hears and answers prayer. When I pray to God, he bows down his ear from heaven to hear what his children say. When a man calls upon the name of the Lord, something happens to him. He becomes a Christian. He is saved. God forgives his sin, writes his name in the Book of Life, and keeps him forever. There is just one way—a plain, simple, and precious way to be saved. If I trust him, he saves me. If I ask him, he comes into my heart. If I confess his name openly and publicly, he writes my name in the Book of Life. He confesses me before the angels in heaven. Praise God!

If the way cost money, some of us might not be able to pay. If the way demanded deep, philosophical erudition, some of us might not be able to pass the examination and we would fail. My brother, if the way demanded holiness, some of us might be eternally lost for we have been so sinful in our lives. But God made it that a child could be saved. God made it that a big, strong, hardened sinner could be saved. I have seen it happen a thousand times. God made it that any one of us can be saved. Just trust Jesus, call on the name of the Lord, and God will come into your heart.

> If you are tired of the load of your sin,
> Let Jesus come into your heart;
> If you desire a new life to begin,
> Let Jesus come into your heart.
>
> Just now your doubtings give o'er;
> Just now reject Him no more;
> Just now throw open the door;
> Let Jesus come into your heart.

LEILA N. MORRIS

7.

The Blood of the Cross

Almost all things are by the law purged with blood; and without shedding of blood is no remission (Heb. 9:22).

The secular and material world is bold and blatant in its rejection of the gospel of atoning blood. They refuse and repudiate the whole message of redemption, stating their opposition bluntly, rudely, and brutally. They say if we have tractors to move mountains, we do not need faith. If we have penicillin, we do not need prayer. If we have positive thinking, we do not need salvation. If we have the state, we do not need the church. If we have manuals on science, we do not need the Bible. If we have an Edison or an Einstein, we do not need Jesus. They define life altogether in secular and material nomenclature.

The Christian Religion Is a Message of Redemption

The gospel of the Son of God addresses itself to a far deeper need of humanity than penicillin, government, or manuals of science. The Christian faith addresses itself to the need for regeneration, the forgiveness of sins, a new life, a new heart, a new way, and a new day. The religion of Jesus Christ is one of deliverance and redemption from the judgment of sin. You see that in the very definition and description of the faith itself. The Christian faith is not, in the first place, an ethic, although it is

75

ethical. It is not in the first place a theology, although it is theological. It is not in the first place reformational, although it has social, cultural, and political overtones. The religion of Jesus Christ is first, foremost, and always redemptive. He was delivered for our offenses, and he was raised for our justification (Rom. 4:25). You can see that in the aegis, the sign, and the symbol of the Christian religion.

The sign of the Christian faith is not a burning bush. It is not two tables of stone bearing the Ten Commandments. It is not a seven-branched lampstand. It is not a halo above a submissive head. It is not even a golden crown. The sign and the aegis of the Christian faith is always a cross—a cross in all of its naked hideousness, as the Romans would have it; the cross in all of its philosophical irrationality, as the Greeks would have it; but the cross in all of its saving power and efficacy, as Paul would have it. "God forbid that I should glory, save in the cross of our Lord Jesus Christ" (Gal. 6:14). This is the very epitome and summation of the redemptive message of Christ.

Have you been to Jesus for the cleansing power?
Are you washed in the blood of the Lamb?
Are you fully trusting in His grace this hour?
Are you washed in the blood of the Lamb?

ELISHA A. HOFFMAN

The Descent and Sufferings of Our Lord

Our minds can hardly enter into the most significant and dramatic of all of the events in human history— the descent of our Lord from the highest glory to the lowest humiliation, the immeasurable distance between his throne in heaven and the ignominy of his cross in the earth. Down and down and down did the Lord descend until he was made in the likeness of a man, made out of the dust of the ground, a slave, poor even among the poor. He was finally executed in a manner reserved for the criminal, raised between heaven and earth, as though he were rejected by men and scorned by God, reviled and abused. As though abuse were not vile enough, they covered him with spittle. As though spittle were not contemptuous enough, they plucked out his beard. As though to pluck out his beard were not brutal enough, they crowned him with thorns. As though the thorns were not sharp enough, they drove great nails through his hands and his feet. As though the nails did not pierce deeply enough, they thrust him through with a Roman spear, and the red, crimson of his life poured out. Even the sun in the sky refused to look upon such shame and suffering.

> Well might the sun in darkness hide,
> And shut his glories in,
> When Christ the mighty Maker died
> For man, the creature's sin.

ISAAC WATTS

What is the crucifixion of the Son of God on the cross? What happened on Golgotha, on Calvary? Is this a dramatic play like the *Agamemnon* of Aeschylus, or the tragedy of Shakespeare's *Macbeth* or *King Lear?* Is it a tragedy like Eugene O'Neill's *The Strange Interlude?* What is this that is happening on Calvary? Is it a historical tragedy like Socrates drinking the hemlock or Julius Caesar murdered

at the foot of the statue of Pompey? Is it like the assassi-
nation of President Lincoln in Ford's Theater or like the
tragedy that brought a cloud over Dallas in the assassina-
tion of President John Kennedy? What is this that happened on Calvary?

The Crucifixion Is the Judgment of God
Upon Our Sin

The death of Christ on the cross is the fruit and the
result of our sins. Who killed the Lord Jesus? Who executed the Prince of Glory? Who nailed him to the cross
where he suffered until he died? Whose fault is that?

So many would answer, "God did it." Like Job's wife
said to him when he fell into abject suffering, "Curse
God and commit suicide." It is God's fault. He did it.

There are others who would say: "It is his own fault.
He should have been a better manager. Had he been
smart, he would not have been nailed to that tree. It is
his own fault."

There are those who would say: "It is Judas' fault.
He sold him for thirty pieces of silver. He betrayed him.
It is Judas' fault. He did it."

There are those who say to this day: "It is the Jews'
fault. They delivered him. They accused him. They en-
compassed his execution. It is their fault. They did it."

There are those who would say: "It is the Roman soldiers' fault. They are guilty of the death of the Lord.
They did it. Who drove those nails through his hands?
They did it. Who thrust that spear into his side? They
did it. Who raised him up between the earth and the
sky? The Roman soldiers did it. They killed him."

It is remarkable that each one disavows the guilt of
the Lord's crucifixion. When Pilate was recalled, he committed suicide, and they flung his body into Lake Lucerne.

That is why just beyond the city of Lucerne there is a tall, towering mountain called Mt. Pilatus, Mt. Pilate. Legend says that in the mist of the twilight of every evening, the peasants see Pontius Pilate rise from the depths of the sea and wash his hands in the clear blue water of Lake Lucerne. "I am guiltless of the blood of this just man. I did not do it."

Then the Jews did it. They are Christ-killers. They crucified him. Without exception, the Jew cries, "Would you bring the blood of this man upon us and upon our children? We did not do it."

Then surely it was the Roman soldiers. They executed him. But the Roman soldiers would stand in attention before you and say: "We are men under authority, and we but carried out the mandates and the commandments of the Roman government. We are soldiers obeying orders. We did not do it."

Then who did? Who is responsible for the crucifixion of the Son of God? Who ultimately must stand at the judgment bar accused?

It must be that we all had a part. My sins pressed upon his brow that crown of thorns. My sins drove through his hand those jagged nails. My sins thrust that spear into his heart. My sins nailed the Lord Jesus to the tree. That is the first meaning of the death of our Lord. It is the fruit and the judgment upon our sins.

The Death of Christ Is the Atonement of God for Our Sins

What is the meaning of the death of our Lord? This is God's redemption for our souls. This is God's way for our salvation. This is God's answer to our sins. This is the Lord's reply to Job when Job cried, "I have sinned, O God, what shall I do?" This is the answer to the cry of Macbeth, "Will all great Neptune's ocean wash this blood Clean from my hands?" This is the reply of the ancient old-time hymn that our forefathers used to sing:

What can wash away my sin?
Nothing but the blood of Jesus;
What can make me whole again?
Nothing but the blood of Jesus.

Oh! precious is the flow
That makes me white as snow;
No other fount I know,
Nothing but the blood of Jesus.

ROBERT LOWERY

What is the meaning of that cross? This is the lamb slain from before the foundation of the world. This is the blood of the Passover Lamb, for the Lord had said, "When I see the blood, I will pass over you." This is the Suffering Servant of Isaiah 53:6, "The Lord hath laid on him the iniquity of us all." This is the great redemption of the Lord God through all time and history. This is the pivotal moment in human story toward which all God's sovereign efforts finally found their ultimate consummation.

So Jesus bowed his head on the cross and cried, "It is finished!" The drops of blood that poured out from the cross to the dust of the ground whispered to the grass, saying, "It is finished!" The grass whispered to the herbs, "It is finished!" The herbs whispered to the trees, "It is finished!" The trees whispered to the birds in the branches, "It is finished!" The birds spiraling upwards to the clouds cried, "It is finished!" The clouds

spoke to the stars in the sky, "It is finished!" The stars
in the sky cried to the angels in heaven, "It is finished!"
The angels in glory went up and down the streets of
the heavenly city echoing this glad refrain, "It is finished!" The crucifixion of our Lord was God's redemption
for the sin of the world.

The Cross Is the Message of Our Salvation

This is not only the death of our Lord, this is not
only the result and the judgment upon our sin, it is not
only God's redemptive plan for the ages, but the cross
is the symbol of our hope in glory. In the words of John
McCrae:

> In Flanders fields the poppies blow,
> Between the crosses, row on row.

Wherever men have fallen in the faith, there will you
see a cross placed by the grave. It is a sign of our faith,
of our promised heaven in the world to come. The arms
of that cross are extended wide, wide as the world is
wide. As far as the West goes West and the East goes
East, just so far are the arms of the cross extended. In
their embrace, all of us can find refuge, forgiveness, salvation, and hope. This hath God done for us.

Experiences in the beginning of my pastoral ministry
made such indelible impressions on me. One of those
experiences that I shall never forget was my first funeral.

In my little country church was a poor tenant farmer
and his wife. They were young people who had been
married just a little while. They had their first baby, a
little boy. They sent for me because their baby was so
tragically ill. I went to a poor shack of a house, in the
days of the depression. In the middle of the room lay a

little baby in convulsions. As I watched sorrowfully, the baby died.

We held the memorial service. After the service, they took the little casket and put it on the bed of a truck. The couple could not afford any kind of service. In my little car, next to me sat the little mother, and on the other side the young father.

As we drove down the country road following the truck which bore the casket, the mother began to cry unconsolably. The young husband put his arm around her, and holding her as near and dear as he could, he said: "There, there, sweetheart. Do not cry. Jesus has our little boy, and he will take care of him for us. Some day he will give him back to us again." At the cemetery we buried the casket in a little grave with a barbed-wire fence around it. Do you know what we placed at the end of that little mound? We placed a cross and drove it into the ground.

The cross is a sign of our hope, our faith, our commitment to Jesus. Every word that he said will he faithfully keep. Every promise that he made will be faithfully kept for us. No word of our Lord will fall to the ground. He is able and mighty to save. That is our Lord, our Savior, our Redeemer, who died for our offenses and was raised for our justification. With what infinite gladness, gratitude, praise, and thanksgiving does the Christian lift up his head in the name of the Lord who died for us, who is able to save us, and who some day will present us before the throne of his glory without spot or blemish, washed clean and white in the blood of the Lamb!

8.

Following Jesus
unto Death

Verily, verily, I say unto thee, When thou wast young, thou girdedst thyself, and walkedst whither thou wouldest; but when thou shalt be old, thou shalt stretch forth thy hands, and another shall gird thee, and carry thee whither thou wouldest not.

This spake he, signifying by what death he should glorify God. And when he had spoken this, he saith unto him, Follow me.

Then Peter, turning about, seeth the disciple whom Jesus loved following; which also leaned on his breast at supper, and said, Lord, which is he that betrayeth thee?

Peter seeing him saith to Jesus, Lord, and what shall this man do?

Jesus saith unto him, If I will that he tarry till I come, what is that to thee? follow thou me (John 21:18–22).

The twenty-first chapter of John is an addendum, an appendix which is added to the Gospel. The Gospel plainly reaches an incomparable and glorious climax in chapter 20 of the book with the marvelous confession of doubting Thomas who cries, saying, "My Lord, and my God." Then John wrote a benedictory sentence:

Many other signs truly did Jesus in the presence of his disciples, which are not written in this book: But these are written, that ye might believe that Jesus is the Christ, the Son of God; and that believing

ye might have life through his name (John 20:30–
31).

That closes the book. What happened apparently was
this. As you know, John lived a whole generation after
the martyrdom of Simon Peter. Simon was martyred
sometime between A.D. 66 and 67. In A.D. 100 the apostle
John, who wrote the Apocalypse, was still living in Ephesus. The Synoptic Gospels, Matthew, Mark, and Luke,
leave Peter in a bad light. He is denying that he even
knows the Lord, quailing before a little maid who says,
"You are one of his disciples; you even talk like him."
Peter denies the Lord, goes out, and weeps bitterly. That
is the way that we leave Peter in the Synoptic Gospels.
John writes a tribute to his old friend, Simon Peter, who
has now been dead for thirty or more years. That tribute
to Simon Peter is the twenty-first chapter of John. The
story goes like this.

After the Lord was raised from the dead, he appeared
unto the disciples in Jerusalem and asked them to meet
him at an appointed mountain in Galilee. Simon Peter
and the disciples had not yet been given the Great Commission. They had no idea of the future of the grace
and age of the church. They were just in Galilee waiting
for that appointed rendezvous with the Lord. While they
were in Galilee waiting, Simon Peter said to the other
six disciples with him: "I am going back to my old business. I am going back to the boats, to the sea, to the
fish, and to the old world. I used to make a living for
my wife and my family, and I am going back to the
old business." Simon Peter was a natural leader of men.
What he did, they all did. So the other six disciples in
Galilee said, "Simon Peter, we are going with you." So
they are back on the lake in the old boat, at the old

nets, at the old business, in the old life. They are back as they were before.

In the gray mist of the morning, John and the disciples see an indistinct, shadowy figure on the shore. Whoever that is calls to the men in the boat and says, "Have you caught anything?"

They call back, "No."

Whoever that is on the shore says to them, "Take your net, put it on the other side of the boat, and you will catch fish."

They lower the net on the other side just a few feet away and catch a great draft of fish. When they do that, John, the disciple whom Jesus loved, says to Simon Peter: "Simon Peter, do you know who that is on the shore? That is the Lord."

Simon Peter, hearing that it was the Lord, jumps into the sea and swims to the shore. The other disciples remain struggling with that big draft of fish.

Then the Lord says to Simon Peter, "Bring up the catch."

That is the reason I know that Simon Peter was a big fisherman. Those six disciples were struggling with that catch of fish, but Simon Peter went down into the sea and pulled up the net by himself. When they came to shore, there the Lord stood over a morning breakfast all prepared. When the Lord and the disciples had dined, the Lord turned to Simon Peter and said, 'Simon, son of Jonah, lovest thou me more than these?"

Simon Peter replies, "Lord, you know that I love you."

Then the Lord replies, "Feed my lambs."

The Lord then asks Peter a second time. The second time Peter avows his devotion to the Lord and the Lord says, "Shepherd my flock." Then the Lord asks Peter a third time, "Simon, son of Jonah, do you really love me?"

Simon Peter, grieved because the Lord asked the third time, says: "Lord, you know all about me. You know that I love you."

Then the Lord said, "Feed my sheep." Then follows the prophecy:

> Verily, verily, I say unto thee, When thou wast young, thou girdedst thyself, and walkedst whither thou wouldest: but when thou shalt be old, thou shalt stretch forth thy hands, and another shall gird thee, and carry thee whither thou wouldest not.
>
> This spake he, signifying by what death he should glorify God (John 21:18–19).

That is, Simon Peter was to die by the outstretched hands; he was to die by crucifixion.

When the Lord had spoken of the form of death that Simon Peter should suffer, he said to Simon, "Follow me."

When Peter followed the Lord to crucifixion unto death, he turned around and saw John following also. Simon Peter said: "Lord, you asked me to follow you unto crucifixion and to death. But what about John?"

The Lord said to him, "If I will that he never dies, that he never suffers, that he is never to be crucified, what is that to thee? Follow thou me."

So John closes his addendum with the picture of Simon Peter faithfully following the Lord unto crucifixion and death. What a tribute from one friend to another!

A Giving Up

What is it to love the Lord supremely, above all else in the world? First of all, it is a giving up. "When they had dined, Jesus saith to Simon Peter, Simon, son of Jonas,

lovest thou me more than these?" Practically every com-
mentary will say that the Lord is asking Simon Peter,
"Simon, son of Jonas, lovest thou me more than these
other disciples love me?" How could Simon answer a
question like that? Would the Lord ask Simon such a
question? In the Greek the meaning of the Lord's word
is not ambiguous. The Lord asked Simon Peter, "Simon,
son of Jonas, lovest thou me more than these—the world,
and all that is in it? Simon, if you do, I am asking you
to give it up and follow me." To love the Lord supremely
is first and always a giving up. There is no one who is
a Christian and there is no one who ever follows the
Lord but shall know the truth of that avowal. To be a
Christian, to follow Jesus, and to love the Lord supremely
is always a giving up. Sometimes it is a giving up of
what is in our sight a small and inconsequential thing,
some little habit, practice, or compromise, but it destroys
our witness for the Lord.

In one of the churches I pastored there was a man
who had a beautiful jewelry store. I was in the store
visiting with him. He had on his finger a very large diamond. I remarked upon the beauty and the enormous
size of that precious gem. He took it off and flung it
on the counter and said, "It is worthless."

I said, "What, that beautiful diamond is worthless?"

He said, "Yes, pick it up and look at it."

I picked it up and saw that it had coal specks all through
it. The diamond was practically worthless.

That is the way with so many Christian lives. They
have dark spots, coal spots, carbon spots in them. What
otherwise could be a magnificent witness for the Lord
is ruined by some little worldly practice. To love Jesus
supremely means to give it up. "But you do not understand, Pastor. This is all right for me. I am not hurt by

it." Maybe not, but your influence is, your Christian testimony is, and if you love Jesus supremely, you will give it up. That is the first response of following Jesus unto death. It is a giving up. Be it small, inconsequential, worldly practices or the deepest, traumatic costs and experiences of human life, we are to give it up for Jesus' sake.

The Acceptance of a Responsibility

To follow the Lord and love him supremely is the acceptance of a responsibility. "Simon, lovest thou me? Take care of my lambs. Simon, lovest thou me? Shepherd my flock. Take care of my sheep." Loving Jesus and following our Lord is always the acceptance of a responsibility. "But Pastor, you do not understand. Do you mean that I, big man as I am, am to try to help with these little children, these little lambs?" What is the matter with a big strong man loving little children? Jesus did. He took them in his arms and blessed them. The mothers delighted in bringing their children to him. What is the matter with a man being a superintendent of a nursery department? What is the matter with a man working with our little children? That is what it is to love Jesus supremely, the acceptance of a responsibility. Jesus said that we are to minister to our little ones first. In building a church, a Sunday School, or any kind of an educational ministry, we ought to start with the little ones. I have never seen a little baby come to church by himself. When you get a baby, you get a mother, a father, a grandmother, a grandfather, the aunts, the uncles, and all kinds of people enlisted and involved in the church. When you interest yourself in a child, you will interest the whole family in the work, way, and will of God. "Feed my lambs. Take care of my little ones. Shepherd my sheep."

All of us have some kind of a gift. Each one of us
has a gift, although my gift may be very menial and
small, apparently insignificant and inconsequential. But
we all have a gift. We all can do something. Maybe the
most I can do is raise the window, sweep a floor, or
stand on the street to show somebody where to park
or help a mother out of the car. All of us can do something. Whatever we can do, we ought to do. That is
what makes the house of God glorious. There are great
stones in the foundation of the church that nobody will
ever see. There are little nails in the top of the roof that
nobody will ever see. But it takes that big stone in the
earth, the little nail in the roof, and all of the many
parts to raise the structure that we call the sanctuary
of God. We all have a contribution to make, and when
we love Jesus supremely, we are happy to make it.
"Lovest thou me? Feed my lambs. Take care of my
sheep." To love Jesus is the acceptance of a responsibility.

Faithfulness unto Death

Loving Jesus, following the Lord, is a faithfulness unto
death. The Lord said:

> Verily, verily, I say unto thee, When thou wast
> young, thou girdedst thyself, and walkedst whither
> thou wouldest: but when thou shalt be old, thou
> shalt stretch forth thy hands, and another shall gird
> thee, and carry thee whither thou wouldest not.
> This spake he, signifying by what death he should
> glorify God (John 21:18–19).

We glorify God in crucifixion? We glorify God in suffering? There is no way that a Christian glorifies God
so brilliantly, so spiritually, and so triumphantly as when

he is in a great agony of suffering or brokenness of heart!
My dear people, anybody can sing when everything is
going his way. Even the infidel is happy when he has
the world for himself. But how do you do when the
evil day comes? How do you do when sorrow comes?
When trouble comes, then do you sing, then do you
glorify God? The Book says that we glorify God in our
trouble, in our suffering, and in our crucifixion. "This
spake he, signifying by what death he should glorify
God." It is how you do in an evil day that determines
the nature and the quality of your Christian faith and
the power and impact that you have upon the world.
Let me show you.

One time Satan and the Lord Jehovah got into an argu-
ment over a man down here in the world. The Lord said:
"See my servant, Job? He is the best man in all the world.
Look at him."

Satan said: "Oh, yes? Well, no wonder. Look at the
hedge you have built around him. You have crowned
him with every prosperity. Look at his flocks, his herds,
his fields, his family, his house, and the wealth you have
poured out upon him. No wonder he glorifies God."

The Lord said, "Are you saying that Job serves me
for what he gets out of it?"

Satan replies: "Yes, he serves you for what he gets
out of it. Take away what he has, and he will curse
you to your face."

God says, "Satan, do you believe that?"

"Yes," replies Satan. "Take away what he has and he
will curse you to your face."

God says, "Fine, just go down there and take everything that he has away, and I say that he will still glorify
my name."

So Satan went down, and he took away everything

that Job had, burned it up with fire, blew it away with the wind, struck it with lightning from the sky, and even killed his children. Old Job looked on the devastation as far as his eyes could see and said: "The Lord gave, and the Lord has taken away. Blessed be the name of the Lord."

God said to Satan: "See, is not that what I said? He is not serving me for what he gets out of it. Look at Job. He is glorifying my name in great despair."

Satan said: "Yes, but skin for skin. He is still well. He is still strong. He is still in health. You let me touch *him,* and he will curse you to your face."

"Oh?" says God to Satan. "Do you think that Job is serving me because I keep him well and strong?"

"Yes," said Satan. "You let me touch him, and he will curse you to your face."

God says to Satan, "You go down and touch him, only spare his life."

Satan went down and afflicted Job with boils from the top of his head to the soles of his feet. It felt good to Job when even a dog would come and lick his sores. Do you know what he did? He sat in an ash heap afflicted in agony and said, "Though he slay me, yet will I trust him."

That is the way to glorify God! You do not glorify God when you are singing songs and everything is going your way. You do not glorify God when the whole world is yours and all that is in it. You glorify God when you praise his name and your heart is broken, when you praise the name of God and you hurt; every bone aches, you are in distress, you are sick, and you are down. "Bless his name!"

Why, my brethren, I think that the most obvious thing in the world is the little sentence that follows the incar-

ceration of Paul and Silas. After they were beaten, after
they were cruelly scourged by Roman rods, they were
thrust in an inner dungeon, their feet were fastened in
stocks, and their hands were locked in manacles. At midnight, with the blood pouring down their beaten backs,
the Book says, "Paul and Silas prayed and sang praises
to God." And now the obvious, "And the prisoners heard
them." No wonder the prisoners heard them! I would
have heard them. One could not help but hear their singing. Beaten, in stocks, in chains, manacled in the midnight
hour with the blood pouring down their backs, there
are Paul and Silas singing songs of praise to God. We
glorify the Lord in our trouble and in our trial. That is
what it is when we are following Jesus faithfully and
loving him supremely.

A Personal Accountability

Following Jesus is a personal accountability. Peter said
to the Lord, "Lord, you say that I am to follow thee
unto crucifixion and unto death? Lord, what about John,
what about him?"

And the Lord replied, "If I will that he tarry till I come,
what is that to thee? follow thou me" (John 21:22). Following Jesus, loving him supremely, faithfully following
unto death is a personal accountability.

There are times when in a decision I make, I take the
whole church into confidence. There are times in the decision that I make, I will take the deacons into confidence.
There are times in a decision that I make that I take
the circle of the family into confidence. But there are
times when my soul is alone and naked before God and
the decision is made before the Lord alone. A personal
accountability, something just between God and me, a

personal commitment and a personal decision.

Many years ago the financial administrator of a world-wide institution in the city of Dallas came to me, a member of our church, and said, "Pastor, God has called me to preach, and I must resign my place and follow the call of the Lord."

I said to him: "Listen, you forget that. First of all, you are accustomed to an affluent life, and the life of the minister, for the most part, is one of poverty. He has the lowest paid profession in America and many times the most difficult time. You forget that. You are the head of a great institution, you have a wonderful salary, and you are accustomed to all of the things that go with it. You have married a girl out of an affluent home, and she is not accustomed to all of the hardships that go with a young preacher out in a beginning ministry. It will not work. Go back to your job and forget it."

He said, "All right." So he went back to his place. After about two or three months he came to me again and said: "God has called me to preach and I cannot escape the call. I am miserable. God wants me to be a preacher."

I talked to him again and said, "You forget it. Go back home, go back to your job."

After two or three months, he came to me again and said: "I am resigning my place; I am giving my life to be a preacher; and I am going to the seminary to prepare for the ministry."

I said, "God help you. That is the most terrible decision that I know that you could make, but God help you."

So he resigned his place, got everything in order, and went to the seminary. After he had been at the seminary a few months, late at night, there was a knock at the door. I went to the door and there he stood. He said, "Would you mind coming out here and sitting with me in the car?"

I replied, "I would be happy to." So I went out to his car.

He said: "I have the saddest thing to tell you. My wife called me in and said, 'Husband, I am not going to be a preacher's wife. Go kiss the little baby in the cradle good-bye, and kiss these other two children good-bye because when you come back from school tomorrow, I am taking them with me and I am going to my mother's home. I am quitting you, and I am not going to be a preacher's wife!' He said, "When I came back from my classes this afternoon, she was gone, the baby was gone, and the two little girls were gone."

I said: "Is not that exactly what I told you? Did not I tell you that you could not be a preacher, that she would not share that kind of life? Did I not tell you to keep your position and forget about being a preacher?"

He said, "Yes, I know."

Then I said, "You go into the house, pick up the phone, and call that mother's home and get your wife on the phone and tell her that you have given up this idea of being a preacher, you are going back into the business world, and you want her to come and bring the children and start your life all over again."

He said: "No, no. God has called me to preach."

I said: "How are you going to be a preacher? How are you going to be called a pastor of a church? Who is going to call a preacher whose children are orphaned and whose wife has divorced him?"

He said, "Maybe God does not want me to be a pastor of a church."

I said, "Do you mean to tell me that without anybody calling you, without any hope of a church, without anything, that you are still going to be a preacher, losing your wife, losing your children?"

He said: "Yes. God has called me, and I have to be a preacher."

I said, "Well, let us pray."

I prayed for him and saw him drive off and back to the seminary. That was one of the saddest nights I ever experienced, seeing that young fellow drive away, back to the seminary to preach on the streets because he felt that it was God's call for him.

A few months passed and one night there was a knock at the door. I opened the door and there he stood again. He said, "Pastor, would you come out and sit in the car?"

I said, "I will be glad to." So I went out to his car.

He said: "Pastor, I received a telephone call from my wife living at her mother's home. This is what she said, 'Husband, it is as though I had been in a tragic illness, as though I had been terribly sick. It is as though I had lost my mind and my perspective in life. I have found myself; I have found the will of the Lord; and I have found my heart. Please, may I come back and bring our three children with me? I will be your helper and your companion as you study for the ministry and as you preach the gospel.' " He told her, "How happy, welcome dear." Then he said, "Tomorrow she will be back in our little apartment with the three children, and we will finish our work together as I prepare to be a minister of the gospel."

So he finished his work and got his degree at the seminary. Upon a day at one of our Baptist General Convention meetings in Texas, I met him again with his beautiful wife by his side and I said: "How are you doing? Where are you living?"

He said, "I am pastor of a county seat town in West Texas, and God is wonderfully blessing our ministry."

It is a personal accountability. There are just some things between you and God which are inescapable. You are born for yourself and nobody was born for you. You have to accept Jesus for yourself. Nobody can do it for you. Some day you will have to die for yourself. Nobody can die for you. Some day you will be judged for yourself. Nobody can be judged for you. There is one great decision before God which you have to make for yourself; namely, what is God's will for my life? If my father and mother are happy in it, glory, thank thee Lord. If they are not, I still must follow after. If every friend I know and have is against it, if God calls me, it is still my commitment to follow after Jesus unto death.

That is what it is to love Jesus supremely. "Follow me unto death."

9.

Scars for the Lord

From henceforth let no man trouble me: for I bear in my body the marks of the Lord Jesus (Gal. 6:17).

Paul said in Corinthians and in Thessalonians that the sign that an epistle was written by him and not a forgery would be that he would write a concluding salutation and sign it with his own hand. After Paul had dictated his letter through an amanuensis, and he thus did all of his writings, he picked up the pen and wrote a concluding salutation. That is what he did in this letter to the churches in Galatia. He dictated the epistle, then after he had finished the dictation, he wrote a final and concluding word. So he begins: "Ye see how large a letter I have written unto you with mine own hand" (Gal. 6:11). A better translation would be: "See with what large letters I am writing to you with my own hand" (RSV). Paul wrote apparently like a schoolboy in large, block letters. Maybe there was something wrong with his eyes. There are many scholars who suppose that the thorn in the flesh that Paul referred to in 2 Corinthians is the trouble that he had with his eyes. There is reason to believe that, but whether or no, that is the way that he wrote, with large, block letters. Then Paul speaks of the tremendous confrontation that he has in the churches of Galatia with the Judaizers. He finally concludes: "From henceforth let no man trouble me: for I bear in my body the

marks of the Lord Jesus" (v. 17). The Greek word is
stigmata. "For I bear in my body *ta stigmata,*" even more
precisely translated, "For I bear in my body the brand
marks of the Lord Jesus."

On the Western plains where I grew up as a boy, every
rancher then as now had a brand registered. The brand
is his. In the roundup in the spring and in the fall, those
cowmen burned the brand of the mother cow on the
calf. That brand mark identified his herds. Especially was
it vital in the days before barbed wire was invented and
the herds intermingled on those vast prairie lands. Every
ranchman had his brand mark.

When I went through Africa several years ago, I never
saw an African (who was not a Christian) but who had
tribal marks incised in his flesh somewhere on his body,
usually on the cheeks. There were deep, vivid scars which
were tribal scars, tribal marks. This man belonged to a
certain clan, a certain family, a certain tribe. They were
the brand marks. They were the tribal marks of that
family, clan, and tribe.

If the Roman Empire was one thing above everything
else, it was an engine of slavery. In the days of the Roman
Empire, 60 million out of a population of 100 million
were chattel property. They were bond slaves. They had
been bought. They had been taken as prizes in war and
sold.

Had one walked down the streets of Ephesus, Corinth,
Antioch, or Rome in the days of the apostle Paul, three
men out of every five he would have met were slaves,
bond servants.

In the days of the Roman Empire they had a mark
that a slave owner cut in the flesh of his slave. He cut
it in the flesh so that if a slave escaped and ran away,
he could be apprehended, arrested, and returned, and

sometimes even crucified. So the Greeks had a name for that scar, that brand mark of slavery and servitude. The Greek name was singular, *stigma,* plural, *stigmata.* We have taken that word and spelled it out exactly in our English language, "stigma." A stigma to us is "a mark of inferiority." But in the days of the Greco-Roman Empire, it referred to the scar that was cut in the flesh of a slave. It was a mark of his servitude, and that is the word that the apostle Paul uses in this concluding salutation, "For I bear in my body *ta stigmata,* the brand marks, the scars of the Lord Jesus."

I always preach out of the King James Version, but sometimes the beauty of its Elizabethan, Shakespearean language translation hides away the rough, jagged edges of the word that Paul has used. Here is an instance. In Romans 1:1, in Philippians 1:1, in Titus 1:1, the King James Version translated it, Paul, a servant of Jesus Christ. What he wrote was, *Paulos doulos Christou Jesou*—"Paul, a slave of Jesus Christ." He would have no mind but Christ's mind, no will but God's will, no work but that assigned by the Lord. He was a slave of the Lord Jesus Christ, a *doulos,* and as such, he says, "I bear in my body the mark of that servitude." Scars for the Lord.

I wish I could have seen the body of the apostle Paul. Had I been able to have met him and have seen the great livid scars all over his face, I could have asked, "Paul, where did those scars come from?"

He could have replied, "Once I was stoned at Lystra and dragged out for dead." Scars for the Lord, the brand marks of the Lord Jesus.

I wish I could have seen his back, crossed and crisscrossed with deep, ugly scars. I could have asked, "Paul, where did those scars come from?"

He could have replied: "Of the Jews, five times received

I forty stripes save one, and thrice was I beaten with
Roman rods." They are scars for the Lord, the brand
marks, the *stigmata* of the Lord Jesus.

I wish I could have seen his wrists and his ankles with
such large calluses. I could have asked, "Paul, where did
those calluses come from?"

He could have replied, "In prisons and in dungeons
above measure."

It is hard for us to realize that most of the ministry
of the apostle Paul was spent in prison, chained to a
Roman soldier.

He would say: "They are the brand marks of the Lord
Jesus. They are the scars for the Lord, the sign of my
servitude, my slavery."

"But Paul, aren't you boasting? Are not you proud?
Are not you referring to your sufferings and your sacrifice
in order to exalt yourself above your brethren?"

No, for he had just written with his own hand, "God
forbid that I should glory, save in the cross of our Lord
Jesus Christ" (Gal. 6:14).

"Then Paul, why are you writing here about your scars,
about your suffering, about your brand marks? Why are
you speaking of them if you are not boasting?"

The answer is apparent in the letter to the churches
of Galatia. Wherever Paul went, there he was hounded
by Judaizers. You see, Paul preached that a man could
be saved just by trusting the Lord Jesus apart from keeping the law of Moses. But the Judaizers said that Paul
is a false apostle. He was not one of the twelve. The
gospel that he preaches is a false gospel. The Judaizers
said: "You cannot be saved just by trusting the Lord.
You have to be circumcised, and you have to keep all
of the laws of Moses. Having kept the legislation of the
Old Covenant, then one can be saved by trusting Jesus

but not by faith alone." Paul's answer to that is the thunderbolt of the letter to the churches of Galatia. Here Paul is defending his apostleship. In it he avows that he received the message by revelation from Jesus himself. As such, in defense of his gospel and of his apostleship, he speaks of his scars, signs of his servitude, and slavery to the Lord Jesus.

It Is Difficult to Ridicule Great Sacrifice

Somehow it is always difficult to minimize, to deprecate, to ridicule, or to scorn deep devotion and consecration unto death. It is difficult to mock and to scorn the consecration of the faithful followers of Jesus.

On the front page of the *Dallas Morning News,* I once saw one of the most ridiculous pictures that one could ever see. It was a picture of a minister of the British government who was speaking before the University of Glasgow. Those students in Scotland who looked with scorn and disdain upon the British government at that time had come prepared for him.

The minister of the British government was introduced. He came to the podium, to the dais, and prepared to deliver his message. When he stood there, they pelted him with rotten vegetables, rotten eggs, and flour. The picture that I saw was this minister of the British government standing before that large student group in the University of Glasgow covered with rotten vegetables, rotten eggs, and flour from his head to his foot. He looked like a ridiculous figure.

But when I saw that picture, my mind went back to another day and another time in the same university, in the same hall, and on the same platform, only this time, the chancellor of the university introduced to the student group God's missionary, David Livingstone. The

history book that I read said that when the chancellor
had finished introducing David Livingstone, that the
Scotsman stood up and came to the front of the platform
to address the students in the University of Glasgow.
When they saw him, they looked at his hair burned crisp
under the torrid heat of the African sun. They looked
at his body emaciated with jungle fever. They looked
at his right arm hanging limp and useless at his side,
destroyed by the attack of a vicious, African lion. The
book said that when the students saw him, with one
accord they stood up in awe, in silence, and in reverence
before God's missionary.

The Strength Is in Suffering

There is a power in consecration. There is a thrust
and a mark in true dedication that causes the whole world
to bow in silence before it. That is the power of the
gospel of the Son of God. It is in his suffering, it is in
his cross, it is in his sobs, his tears, in his blood that
we have a message of salvation to preach. Take away
the crown of thorns, the prayer of Gethsemane, the suffering, the blood, and we are still in our sins. The power
of the gospel of the Son of God lies in the cross of our
Lord Jesus Christ, in his sufferings for us, in the pouring
out of the crimson of his life unto death.

That is the power of the gospel of Christ. Paul writes,
"God forbid that I should glory, save in the cross of
our Lord Jesus Christ" (Gal. 6:14). That is the power
and the thrust of the gospel message that we preach today. The power of our preaching is found in our consecration, our devotion, and our commitment to the cross
of Christ. The strength of our message and the thrust
and power of our gospel lies in the tears, the blood, the
heart, and the toil that we are willing to dedicate to the

Lord. If I had any observation to make of the modern Christian message, it is that we are weak, frail, feeble, sterile, anemic, and unprofitable because of our unburdened hearts, our unwept tears, our unspoken testimonies, and our unsung songs. The thrust and the power of the message is found in our willingness to pour our lives into it. Scars for the Lord.

I remember picking up the daily paper and reading of one of these crimes that we usually do not discuss. So I briefly, summarily, casually read what had happened here in the city of Dallas and then promptly tried to forget it. A few days later a woman came to my study. She had with her a boy sixteen years old. Looking so sad, she said, "I am sure you know why I have come."

I said: "Mother, I have no idea. I do not know you. I never heard of you. I have never seen you before. Why have you come?"

She said, "I am sure that you have heard of us."

Then I turned to the boy and said, "Son, is your name so-and-so?"

He said, "Yes." He was the boy who committed the crime printed on the front page of that newspaper.

So I said, "Mother, what can I do to help?"

She said: "Last night my boy came into my bedroom, and he fell down at the chair where I was seated and cried, saying, 'Mother, where can I find God? I need God. Mother, where can I learn about God?' " She said to me: "I could not tell him. I did not know how to answer. When I was a little girl, I went to a Methodist Sunday School, but it has been so many years ago, I cannot remember anything that I learned. I went next door, and I said to my sweet neighbor, 'My boy is on his face in my bedroom. He wants to know where he can find God. Would you come and tell him?' The neighbor answered:

'I do not know how to say. I cannot tell him, but I listen
to Brother Criswell every Sunday on the radio. You take
your boy to him, and he will tell your boy how to meet
God, where to find God.'" So the mother said, "I have
brought the boy here for you to tell him how he can
find God."

I turned to the lad first and said: "Son, may I ask you
a few simple questions? One, how long have you lived
in Dallas?"

The boy replied: "I have lived in Dallas all of my life.
I was born here."

I said, "Son, did you ever go to church?"

He said, "No, not one time in my life."

I said, "Son, did you ever hear a sermon?"

He said, "No, sir, not one in my life."

I said, "Son, were you ever in Sunday School?"

He said, "No, never in my life."

I said: "Lad, may I ask you just one other question.
Did anybody, anytime ever invite you to Sunday School
or to church?"

The boy replied, "No, sir, never."

There are over 235 Southern Baptist churches in the
city of Dallas. There are over 1,000 churches in the city
of Dallas. This boy grew up in this city all of the days
of his life, and not one time did anybody anywhere ever
invite him to the Lord, to the Sunday School, or show
any interest in his soul whatsoever! Where are our scars
for the Lord? What are we doing to invite people to
Jesus? Our unspoken testimonies, our unburdened hearts,
our unwept tears, and our unsung songs condemn us
before God.

The Power of Personal Witnessing

Sometimes an experience will happen to you in your
beginning days that change and color all of the afteryears

of your life. I want to tell you of one that changed my life.

In the years of the long ago when I was a youth, I was invited to hold a two-week revival meeting in a church in which I had never met the people or the pastor. So I began preaching the best I could to those people. All the first week, we had a service every morning and every night, and nobody was saved. There was no burden of heart.

All through the second week, every morning and every night, I preached, but there was nobody with burden of heart and nobody saved. On Friday morning of that second week, I stood in the pulpit of that church and asked each one: "Is there anybody that you are praying will be saved? Is there anyone who is a burden on your heart that they might know Christ? Is there anyone that you are expecting to be saved?"

One by one every member of the church shook his head and indicated that there was no one for whom he was praying or burdened. I started to have a broken-hearted and benedictory prayer, and when I did, there was a little mother, a widow seated on the second row who said: "Wait, Brother Criswell, wait! My husband is dead and I am rearing my two boys alone on the farm. My two boys are lost." For the first time somebody wept before the Lord. When she gained her composure, she said, "Oh, that somebody would help me win my two boys to Jesus!"

We had our benediction and then, as the custom was, we all went to eat lunch in a lovely country home. The table was covered with delicious dishes that the hostess had prepared. After the dinner we all went out into the yard and sat down. The people began to visit together. As the time wore on, my heart grew heavier and heavier. Finally, I turned to the pastor and said, "Pastor, did you hear that little woman at the church this morning?"

He said, "Yes."

I said: "Her husband is dead, her two boys are lost, and she is praying that somebody will help win them to Jesus. Did you hear that?"

He said, "Yes."

I said, "What are you going to do about it?"

He said: "Nothing. If the Lord is going to save them, he will save them."

I said, "Do you know where she lives?"

He said, "Yes."

I said: "Would you get one of these men who is here to take me to that poor widow's home? Do not worry about my getting to church tonight. I will find some way."

He said, "Do you want to do that?"

I said, "I want to do that more than anything in the world."

So he asked one of the men to drive me to the widow's farmhouse. I got out at the road and said, "I will walk up to the farmhouse and I thank you for bringing me." So I walked up to the door of that farmhouse and knocked at the door. The mother came to the door. I said: "Sweet mother, I heard what you said this morning. Your two boys are lost, and you are praying that someone would win them to Jesus. I have come to win them to the Lord. Where are your boys?"

She said, "My younger son is milking in the barn, and my older son has not come in yet from the field."

I said: "Mother, you get on your knees and you pray here in the house. I am going to try to win those boys to Jesus."

I went to the barn and there was the younger son milking the cows. I talked to that boy about Jesus. I read to the boy out of the Book of how he could be saved.

I asked him if he wanted to be a Christian, if he wanted God to forgive his sin, and to write his name in the Book of Life. I said, "Son, if you do, take my hand."

I extended my hand and he grasped my hand hard and said, "Yes, I will accept the Lord as my Savior."

I said, "Let us kneel here and pray." We knelt, and I thanked God that the Lord had come into his heart and saved him.

By that time the older son was unhitching the harness from the team of the field. I walked over into the other section of the barn where he was hanging up the harness and I said to him, "Your mother is praying for you that you will be a Christian, and I have come to tell you how." I read to him out of the Bible; I witnessed to him of what Jesus could do when he comes into a young man's life. I asked him if he would take the Lord as his Savior, and if he would, would he take my hand. This boy also grasped my hand. I said, "Son, let us thank God." We knelt down on the barn floor, and I thanked God for saving the young man's life.

That night when I gave the invitation, those two boys came down the aisle together arm in arm. The mother was so glad, she clapped her hands and praised God. They were the only two souls that were saved in that meeting. Nobody else was saved.

When the day was done and I turned my face to the life that lay before me, I said to myself then, and I have said it in my deepest soul ever since, I believe in praying for the lost. I believe in witnessing to the lost. I believe in visiting the lost. I believe in knocking at the door of our people. I believe in personal evangelization, personal soul-winning, personal witnessing, and personal invitation to follow the Lord Jesus. I know that God blesses the church, the family, the Sunday School teacher, the deacon, and the pastor anywhere in the world who will knock at the door, who will invite people to the Lord Jesus, and who will witness to the grace and love of Christ in his life. Our scars for the Lord. "For I bear in my body *ta stigmata* for the Lord Jesus."

10.
The Reality
of the Resurrection

Now I stand and am judged for the hope of the promise made of God unto our fathers:

Unto which promise our twelve tribes, instantly serving God day and night, hope to come. For which hope's sake, king Agrippa, I am accused of the Jews.

Why should it be thought a thing incredible with you, that God should raise the dead? (Acts 26:6–8).

In Acts 25 and 26 there is recorded the apology, the defense of the apostle Paul as he stood trial for his life. He is in Caesarea, having been arrested in the Temple in Jerusalem. In Caesarea for over three years he has been incarcerated. Felix the procurator, having been recalled, and Festus the new governor, having been sent to take his place, finds one of the prisoners named Paul left in the prison. He listens to the prisoner and the charges that are made against him and is most astonished at the accusations.

> When they had been there many days, Festus declared Paul's cause unto the king, saying, There is a certain man left in bonds by Felix:
>
> About whom, when I was at Jerusalem, the chief priests and the elders of the Jews informed me, desiring to have judgment against him.
>
> To whom I answered, It is not the manner of the

Romans to deliver any man to die, before that he
which is accused have the accusers face to face, and
have licence to answer for himself concerning the
crime laid against him.

Therefore, when they were come hither, without
any delay on the morrow I sat on the judgment
seat, and commanded the man to be brought forth.

Against whom when the accusers stood up, they
brought none accusation of such things as I
supposed:

But had certain questions against him of their own
superstition, and of one Jesus, which was dead,
whom Paul affirmed to be alive.

And because I doubted of such manner of questions, I asked him whether he would go to Jerusalem,
and there be judged of these matters.

But when Paul had appealed to be reserved unto
the hearing of Augustus, I commanded him to be
kept till I might send him to Caesar.

Then Agrippa said unto Festus, I would also hear
the man myself. To morrow, said he, thou shalt hear
him.

And on the morrow, when Agrippa was come,
and Bernice, with great pomp, and was entered into
the place of hearing, with the chief captains, and
principal men of the city, at Festus' commandment
Paul was brought forth.

And Festus said, King Agrippa, and all men which
are here present with us, ye see this man, about
whom all the multitude of the Jews have dealt with
me, both at Jerusalem, and also here, crying that
he ought not to live any longer.

But when I found that he had committed nothing
worthy of death, and that he himself hath appealed
to Augustus, I have determined to send him.

Of whom I have no certain thing to write unto my lord. Wherefore I have brought him forth before you, and specially before thee, O king Agrippa, that, after examination had, I might have somewhat to write.

For it seemeth to me unreasonable to send a prisoner, and not withal to signify the crimes laid against him (Acts 25:14–27).

In Acts 26 Paul is making the defense for the faith before Herod Agrippa II. In that defense he says:

Now I stand and am judged for the hope of the promise made of God unto our fathers:

Unto which promise our twelve tribes, instantly serving God day and night, hope to come. For which hope's sake, king Agrippa, I am accused of the Jews.

Why should it be thought a thing incredible with you, that God should raise the dead? (vv. 6–8).

What a poignant question and appeal! Why should you who believe in God think that it would be incredible that the same mighty Jehovah Lord should raise the dead?

It would be trite for me to say that the doctrine of the resurrection of the dead and the grand pronouncement of the resurrection of Jesus from among the dead is literally the dynamic foundation of the Christian faith. The Scriptures say: "If Christ be not risen, then is our preaching vain, and your faith is also vain. . . . ye are yet in your sins. But now is Christ risen from the dead, and become the firstfruits of them that slept" (1 Cor. 15:14,17,20). This is the doctrine, the teaching, and the heralded pronouncement of the resurrection of Christ from the dead!

In the message we shall look at seven incontrovertible

facts of the raising up from the dead of Jesus our Lord:
(1) a philosophical fact, (2) a pragmatic fact, (3) a psychological fact, (4) an ecclesiastical fact, (5) a soteriological
fact, (6) a literary fact, and (7) an experiential fact.

A Philosophical Fact

One of the most poignant and meaningful of all the
verses in the Bible is Romans 1:4. In speaking of Jesus
Christ, Paul uses the word *horizo* from which the English
word *horizon* is derived and refers to "the place marked
out where the earth meets the sky." The verb translated
literally means in the text, "Jesus Christ is marked out
among all mankind." This man is "marked out" to be
the Son of God with power by the Spirit of holiness in
the resurrection from the dead.

It is an incontrovertible fact that in this universe there
is omnipotence, there is power immeasurable. We see
it every day and on every hand. The sun shines by the
fiat of God. The oceans are liquid. The planets in their
orbits are guided by the infinitude of an invisible hand.
In a thousand other ways do we see the immeasurable
power of God in the earth. That power also and no less
reaches down to the morality in which God has created
us in the universe. It is as factual that there is right and
wrong and that we are sensitive to it as that the sun
shines or that the planets swing in their orbits around
it.

The life of our Lord was beautiful, perfect, godly, spiritual, and reverential. He lived a holy and beautiful life,
but that life ended in shame and disgrace. He was crucified and executed as a common felon and an ordinary
criminal. In this vast universe, is that the verdict of right
and morality? Does wrong triumph over right? Do sin,
death, and the grave reign forever? The same Lord God

Almighty who made the sun to shine and the planets to swing in their orbits around it and who created all of the marvelous wonders of life that astonish our eyes is the same Lord God that created our sensitivity to right and wrong. It is impossible, unthinkable that wrong should forever triumph, that truth should forever be in disgrace, and that sin, death, and the grave should have dominion over God's heritage, world without end. There is a philosophical reason that lies back of the resurrection of Jesus Christ and the triumph of goodness over evil, of life over death, and of heaven over hell.

A Pragmatic Fact

The Lord was buried in a winding sheet with one hundred pounds of spices, with a headdress separate and apart, and he was laid in a tomb over which a heavy stone was rolled. That stone was sealed by the seal of the Roman Empire, the highest authority the world had ever known. Not only that, but it was guarded by a Roman guard to see that the Lord stayed dead.

On the third day, the body was gone. The tomb was empty. The graveclothes were undisturbed, but the body had disappeared. What happened to the body of our Lord?

He could have been removed from the grave by human hands or by supernatural hands. If by human hands, he could have been taken from the tomb by two different groups, by his friends or by his enemies. Did the apostles steal his body away? How could they? He was there in a tomb covered by a heavy stone, sealed by the seal of the Roman emperor, and guarded by a contingency of Roman soldiers. Would they have stolen the body away?

The soldiers were there to see to it that no such legendary hallucination could have happened! They were there

to guard the tomb. For them to steal the body is unthinkable. Why, in a few days after the crucifixion of our
Lord, Simon Peter is standing up and announcing to Jerusalem all of the marvelous good tidings that Jesus is raised
from the dead! All it would have taken to have shown
the lie to the preaching of Simon Peter was for his foes
and enemies who crucified the Lord to say: "This man
says that Jesus is alive. Come here." Opening the tomb,
they would exhibit the dead, decaying body of the Son
of God. Why did not they do it? Because there was no
body there to be exhibited. The undisturbed graveclothes
were empty. The body had disappeared. That is a pragmatic fact, undeniable.

A Psychological Fact

We have to account in some way for the miraculous
change in the mind and attitude and spirit and life of
the disciples. On Friday they are cast down in the depths
of despair. Every hope they had entertained had died
when Jesus expired on the cross. They never believed
in a resurrection. They were the ones who had argued
against it. They were the ones who had to be shown.
As one of them said: "I do not believe that he is raised
from the dead unless I put my finger in the print of
the nails and thrust my hand into the riven scar in his
side. I do not believe." Those are the disciples. Yet three
days later, they are flames of fire. They are filling Jerusalem and the whole earth with the heralding and announcement of the good news of the resurrection of Jesus
Christ. How does one account for that? That is a
psychological fact and must be faced. There are three possi-
bilities.

One, they are proclaiming a lie. The disciples stole
his body away and hid it. Now they are saying that he

was raised from the dead. They are preaching a lie.

That is a psychological impossibility. These men are suffering for the faith. They are being executed, crucified, burned at the stake, and cast into boiling caldrons of oil, laying down their lives. Was it for a lie? It is psychologically impossible. Men do not lay down their lives for a lie. Yet every one of those apostles was executed except John who was exiled to die in exposure and starvation.

Two, it was a legend. You mean a legend could develop in three days? It is psychologically unthinkable and unimaginable.

Three, it was a lunatic hallucination. Mary Magdalene said that she saw the Lord raised from the dead. The French critic Renan said, "The dream of a hallucinated woman became the foundation and the hope of the church." Ridiculous! Not only did Mary Magdalene say: "I have seen him. He is raised from the dead." Simon Peter, the two on the way to Emmaus, all of the apostles, the five hundred brethren at once, and James, the Lord's brother also declared that Jesus had risen from the dead. For forty days did they walk with him, see him, and talk with him. Could it be just at that particular time, never before and never after, these hundreds and hundreds were deluded by lunatic hallucinations? It is unthinkable. This is a psychological fact of the marvelous transformation of those disciples from men of despair to men of the preaching of the great faith of Christ for which they laid down their lives.

An Ecclesiastical Fact

Where did the church originate? The church is the most dynamic creation ever born in the history of humanity. How did the church begin and who gave it power?

The first church was composed entirely of Jews. On the day of Pentecost there were three thousand Jews who were added to the faith. In the next chapter there are five thousand *andron,* men, who are now obedient to the faith, which would mean there were at least twenty-five thousand members in the church. In the book of Acts we read that a great multitude of priests have now become obedient to the faith.

In the Old Covenant in the book of Deuteronomy it is written, "For he that is hanged is accursed of God" (21:23). Yet in Jerusalem there are thousands and thousands of Jews who are humble disciples and followers of the Son of God. How does one explain that? That primitive group faced the Greco-Roman world with fearless and bold intrepidity. They challenged the whole system of civilized worship, including every false god in every province of the Roman Empire. That was no small assignment because the hand of the emperor sustained worship, and it was looked upon as a patriotic duty that every citizen of Rome and every slave in the Roman Empire was to bow down before the image of the emperor and place on the flame that burned before his image a small piece of incense. The Christian refused to bow before the emperor and challenged the whole system of religion. The cry in those days became: "The Christians to the lions! The Christians to the stake!"

The Romans fed the Christians to wild beasts, and they burned them with fire. But that primitive church faced the Roman emperor in all of his power and they challenged the whole system of ancient worship. Within a relatively short time they turned the Roman Empire on new hinges and subverted the entire Greco-Roman world of false deity and false worship. Do you know anybody today who is worshiping Neptune? Do you know anybody today who is worshiping Venus, Apollo, or Juno? Do you know anybody today who is building elaborate temples to those false deities? That primitive Christian church subverted the whole civilized world.

A Soteriological Fact

The conversion of Saul of Tarsus was monumental, for he had breathed threatening and slaughter against the people of God, hauled them into prison, and put them to death. Saul, the archenemy of Christ and of the Christian faith, is now preaching the faith that once he destroyed. What happened?

On the road to Damascus above the brightness of the noonday Syrian sun, there appeared to Saul the Son of God. Saul fell at his feet and said:

> Who art thou, Lord? And the Lord said, I am Jesus whom thou persecutest: . . . Arise, and go into the city, and it shall be told thee what thou must do, . . . Go thy way: for he is a chosen vessel unto me, to bear my name before the Gentiles, and kings, and the children of Israel (Acts 9:5,6,15–16).

How does one account for that? Was this man a small man in mind and understanding? There has never lived a greater in mind and in spiritual sensitivity than Saul of Tarsus, Paul, the apostle.

Most of the New Testament is advantageously, summarily written by Paul with no thought of a great literary masterpiece, just writing out of his heart to a church or to a son in the ministry, and yet the words that he writes are Scripture themselves. They are the revelations of God and rise from one literary peroration to another. There is no language beyond and no literature that excels Paul's compositions. This is the man who was converted on the Damascus road.

Not long after the crucifixion of our Lord, about seventeen years later, Paul wrote the letter to the church at Thessalonica. A short time later he wrote the first Corinthian letter. In those letters Paul expresses an infinitely precious hope in the resurrection of Jesus Christ. He names these to whom the Lord appeared.

He names James, the five hundred or more at one time with whom the Lord appeared on an appointed mountain in Galilee; he speaks of the twelve, of Simon Peter, and of the two on the way to Emmaus. When Paul wrote of these events, the people to whom the Lord had appeared were still alive. Any man could have verified the words of the apostle Paul because the witnesses were still living.

The conversion of Paul and the avowals that he writes in his letters are incontrovertible facts. There are thirteen of his letters. With Dr. Luke, Acts, and the epistle to the Hebrews, which many think he wrote, there are sixteen books in the New Testament that come from the heart and life of this great witness, the apostle Paul. It is a soteriological fact, a conversional fact.

A Literary Fact

In the Bible for anyone to read are the four Gospels. There is a literary fact in the substance of those four Gospels to which we usually have never been introduced. In the four Gospels is presented the story of God and man walking and conversing side by side. They do it naturally, dutifully, and harmoniously. That is a literary impossibility. You see, through the centuries great literary giants have tried to place in converse supernatural and natural, gods and men, and what they seek to accomplish is manifestly of a laborious imagination. They never succeed, for what they produce is always fiction.

There is not a school boy but who has been introduced to Greek and Roman mythology. The literary giants, Homer and Euripides, write about gods and men. The writings of Aeschylus and Sophocles and other like ancient Greek authors are manifestly fictitious. They do not in any wise even attempt to portray the truth of reality, but they produce a story, a novel, an imagination.

The greatest literary genius of all time in the English-speaking world is the myriad-minded Shakespeare. In the most outstanding of his tragedies, *Hamlet,* he presents a scene between the ghost and Hamlet, but it is manifestly fictitious. Even Shakespeare is laboring with a heavy imagination trying to make the story appear plausible and reasonable.

In the Bible we read of Deity and humanity talking and walking and visiting and sharing, even eating together in perfect and beautiful harmony. Renan, the French philosopher, said that the most beautiful story in literature is Luke 24 which is the story of the raised, the risen, and the resurrected Lord as he walks with the two saddened disciples on the way to Emmaus and was made known to them in asking the blessing before the breaking of bread. The story is so natural, so beautiful, so simple, and so real. Why?

Because these men are not writing out of prolific and fertile imagination. The men who wrote the four Gospels are writing a plain, simple, beautiful, marvelous, and heavenly truth. They are describing in simple language what had happened: Jesus was raised from among the dead. Jesus, the Savior of our souls, is alive and is blessing the disciples.

An Experiential Fact

There is not a greater fact in human experience than this: Jesus lives. He is more alive today than he ever was. He lives on university campuses. He lives in professorial chairs. He lives in the academic world. He lives in the dark continent of Africa. He lives in the Amazon Jungle. He lives in the Orient. He lives in the great cities of America. He lives in our churches. He lives in our souls, in our homes, and in our hearts. Jesus is alive!

Alexander the Great is dead. I never hear anyone who thinks otherwise. Julius Caesar and Augustus Octavius are dead. Charlemagne is dead. Napoleon is dead. Washington is dead. Lincoln is dead. All of the past greats of this earth are dead. But I meet Jesus the Christ down almost every road. I see him in ten thousand places.

Walking through one of the great museums of the earth, I stood transfixed before a beautiful and moving picture. The artist had drawn the interior of a humble cottage. All the surroundings were poor. Members of an impoverished family are seated around a kitchen table and are bowing their heads in prayer. The father is saying grace at the table. The gifted artist had drawn the Lord Jesus Christ with his hands extended in blessing above the bowed heads. The caption stated, *Christ Among the Lowly.* As I looked at the effective painting, I thought, "How blessed, how faithful, and how true. Christ with his hands extended above the bowed heads of the poor!"

Walking down the streets of Boston, Massachusetts, I walked by Trinity Church. Next to the entrance on the side of the church is a sculptured statue of Phillips Brooks, the famed preacher of Jesus. Back of Phillips Brooks stands Jesus the Christ with his hand on the shoulder of Phillips Brooks.

Looking at the beautiful harbor of Rio de Janeiro on the top of a hill overlooking the entire city is a mammoth statue of Jesus the Christ with his arms extended in blessing.

In the heart of the Amazon Jungle among Stone Age Indians that had known no other thing in their tribal lives but to bathe their hands in human blood, I stood with a Bible in my hand reading the precious truths about Jesus, speaking to their hungry hearts, singing and praying together with them in the name of the Lord.

Men preach the gospel in Australia, Indonesia, Africa, India, Europe, North America, South America, and in the islands of the sea. He is alive! He lives!

With eyes of faith we have seen him. He spoke to me, and with the ears of my soul I heard and I have never been the same since. This is an incontrovertible fact.

There is no attestation today to any truth that is known to humankind more fully authenticated than the fact of the resurrection of Jesus our Lord from among the dead. He is our hope, our Savior, our mediator and intercessor, our great God and coming King!

11.

The Two-fold Mystery
of the Church

We are members of his body, of his flesh, and of his bones.

For this cause shall a man leave his father and mother, and shall be joined unto his wife, and they two shall be one flesh.

This is a great mystery: but I speak concerning Christ and the church.

Nevertheless let every one of you in particular so love his wife even as himself; and the wife see that she reverence her husband (Eph. 5:30–33).

To us a mystery is an enigma, a riddle, something that is beyond our understanding or finding out. In the language of the days of our Lord and of his apostles, the word *mystery*, in Greek, *musterion*, was an altogether different thing. If one was inducted into the mystery religions, the secrets of the religion were only revealed upon his initiation into the religion. A similar arrangement can be found in the Masonic Lodge in which there are secrets which are revealed to those who are initiated into the lodge. That is the word *musterion* in the Greek world which refers to "a secret that is unknown until it is revealed to the initiated." In the Bible the word *musterion* was used to refer to "a secret that God has kept in his heart until he reveals it unto his holy apostles." So the apostle Paul writes in the text: "This is a great mystery: but I speak concerning Christ and the church" (v. 32). It is a secret that God kept in his heart until he revealed it to his holy apostles.

There are many facets of the meaning of the mystery of the church. For example, the mystery refers to the whole dispensation of grace, this age of the Holy Spirit. The apostles alone knew it. None of the prophets ever saw it. The church is not mentioned in the Old Testament. It was a secret God kept in his heart until he revealed it to his holy apostles. This is the hiatus, the great interlude between the sixty-ninth and seventieth weeks of the book of Daniel.

The Mystery of the Church Is Two-fold

We are going to look at the *musterion* of the church, which is two-fold. First, it is two-fold in its origin. Where did the church come from? In Ephesians 5, Paul says that the church was born in the sobs, the cries, the wounds, the suffering, the blood, and the death of Christ. It was taken out of the scar in his side. In the passage of our text, Paul quotes Genesis 2:23–24. In that story in the book of Genesis, the Lord God caused a deep sleep to come upon Adam. God took out of the side of Adam and made Eve. The word is translated in the King James Version "rib," but in no other place in the Bible is that word ever translated "rib." For forty years I have been unable to discover where the word *rib* originated. Everywhere else in the Bible the word used is "side," such as the "side of the tabernacle," the "side of the ark," or the "side of the altar." The translation in Genesis should also be "side." God took out of the side of Adam and created Eve and brought her to Adam. When Adam saw her, he said: "This is now bone of my bones and flesh of my flesh. She shall be called *Isha* because she was taken out of *Ish.* She shall be called 'woman' because she was taken out of 'man.' " Paul uses the creation of Eve out of Adam's side as the imagery of the creation of the church.

As God took Eve out of the side of Adam from near his heart, so the Lord took the church out of the side of our crucified Lord. We are born in the sobs, the sufferings, the crucifixion, and the death of our Lord. We are taken out of the scar in his side; therefore, Paul says: "We are members of his body, of his flesh, and of his bones." When we become Christians, we are added, we are baptized into the body of Christ.

The Church Is Born in the Word

Second, Paul says that we are not only taken out of the side of our Lord and not only born out of his sufferings and his crucifixion, but we are born in the Word. He uses an amazing word that one would never see in the English translation. He says, "Christ also loved the church, and gave himself for it; that he might sanctify and cleanse it with the washing of the water by the word." The Hebrew word is *kiyor*, the Greek word is *loutron;* the English translation is "washing." If we were to translate the word exactly, the word would be "laver." The "laver" between the altar and the door of the sanctuary was the place where the priest washed himself as he came to present himself before the Lord.

We are born in the Word of Christ. The apostles say that the church is born out of the "washing," the *kiyor*, the *loutron*, the "laver" of the Word of God. We are born in the Word of Christ. No one is ever introduced into the kingdom of our Savior who is not born *by* the Word and *in* the Word. That is what the Lord referred to when in John 3:5 he says, "Except a man be born of water and of the Spirit, he cannot enter into the kingdom of

God." That is, except a man be born of the Word, of the gospel message, and of the regenerating power of the Holy Spirit of God, he can never be saved. No man is ever saved apart from the preaching of the Word of God. We are born by the Word, in the Word, through the Word. "Faith cometh by hearing, and hearing by the word of God" (Rom. 10:17).

For example, when the persecutor Saul of Tarsus was on his way to Damascus to haul into prison those who were calling upon the name of the Lord Jesus, the Lord appeared to him in the way. Saul fell down at his feet and said, "Lord, what wilt thou have me to do?"

The Lord Jesus said, "Go into the city, and there it shall be told thee what thou must do." Why did not Jesus tell him what to do? He is standing there before him face to face. No man comes into the will of God apart from the delivery of the message of another man.

Another instance can be found in Acts 10 when an angel appears unto Cornelius and essentially says: "Your prayers are heard, your alms are seen. Send down to Joppa for one Simon who will come and tell thee words whereby thee and thy house may be saved." Why did not the angel tell him the words whereby he and his house could be saved? The angel was standing before him; the angel was speaking to him, and yet he says, "Send down for Simon who will come and tell thee words whereby thee and thy house may be saved." No man is ever saved apart from the preaching of the gospel of the Son of God. That is why the blood of the entire world is upon our hands. Without us, they cannot be saved. Romans 10:14 tells us: "How then shall they call on him in whom they have not believed? and how shall they believe in him of whom they have not heard? and how shall they hear without a preacher?" (Rom. 10:14).

The whole world is depending upon us for the delivery of the Word of the Lord. This is the mystery, the *musterion*, the origin of the church. It is born out of the suffering side of our Lord, and it is born out of the preached Word of the living God.

The Ordinances of the Church Are Two-fold

The ordinances of the church are two-fold. There is an initial ordinance, the ordinance of baptism. By the Holy Spirit we are baptized into the body of Christ. The imagery of that is seen in our baptism in water. Upon our confession of faith in the Lord Jesus, we are baptized in the name of the triune God. "See," said the Ethiopian eunuch to the evangelist Philip, "here is water. What doth hinder me to be baptized?" The first thing that someone who is born again will say is: "I want to be baptized just as it says in the Book, just as our Lord was baptized, just as all of the apostles were baptized. I want to be baptized, buried with the Lord, raised with the Lord in the likeness of his living, glorious resurrection." This is the first and the initial ordinance of the church.

The second ordinance is recurring, the breaking of bread and the sharing of the cup. "This is my body which is given for you. This is my blood which is shed for the remission of sins. As oft as you eat the bread and drink the cup, you do show forth, you portray, you dramatize the Lord's death till he come." I know what that means when the Lord says, "This is my body and this is my blood." He was standing before the apostles when he avowed it. Therefore, I know that he does not mean, "This is my actual body and this is my actual blood." The Lord's Supper represents, it brings to mind, it is a memorial. "This do in remembrance of me," that we might not forget the sacrifice he made for our sins.

There was a very wealthy man in the city of Dallas who belonged to our church. I was visiting in his home, a beautiful, palatial mansion. He took me to the library, and on the wall of the library was an oval picture of an old-fashioned girl. The way her hair was styled and her dress was made portrayed a long-ago period. She looked to be about eighteen years of age. As I stood by the side of this distinguished Dallas businessman, he pointed to the picture and said, "Pastor, that is my mother." As he looked at the picture, he said: "I never saw her. She died when I was born. The first thing I want to do after I see Jesus when I am in heaven is to see my sainted mother." He was very moved as he stood there and talked to me about his mother whom he had never seen. I could have answered in ridicule and sarcasm: "Sir, you mean that is your mother? That is just ink, cardboard, and paper. That is not your mother." I did no such thing. It would have been rude and brutal for me thus to have thought such a thing. I knew exactly what he meant. When he said, "Pastor, this is my mother," he meant: "This represents my mother. This brings back to me the memory of my sainted mother who gave her life for me, whom I shall see someday in heaven."

It is exactly that with this recurring ordinance. "This is my body, broken for you. This is my blood, shed for you." I know what the Lord means. "This represents my suffering on the cross. This represents the crimson of my life poured out upon the ground. This do in remembrance of me. Every time you observe the Lord's Supper, let it bring back to your heart the memory of my death in your behalf and the promise that some day you will see me in glory."

There Are Two Ordained Officers of the Church

There are two ordained officers of the church. The first ordained officer of the church is the *presbuteros*, the *episkopos*, or the *poimen*. In the Bible all three words are used interchangeably to refer to the same office. The *presbuteros*, translated "elder," refers to the respect that the congregation is to have for their spiritual leader. The word *episkopos*, "overseer," refers to the function, the assignment, the godly work of the pastor in the church. The *poimen* is the Greek word for "shepherd." The pastor is to be the shepherd of the flock. He is to love the people and to seek after and care for their highest spiritual welfare. All three of those words are used interchangeably to refer to the same officer.

Presbuteros, "elder," refers to the dignity of his office. Anytime that one finds a congregation that looks upon their pastor as a cheap hireling, there will he find a church in which the seeds of disintegration are already growing. There is no such thing as a great and wonderful church but that treats their pastor and looks upon him with deepest respect and reverence. That is why I think this church is the greatest of all the churches in the world. For forty-seven years this church looked with love and deepest respect upon the far-famed pastor, Dr. George W. Truett. When Dr. Truett died and they called me, I was forty-three years younger than Dr. Truett, but I inherited that same deference, love, and respect that this great church had for that mighty preacher. They called Dr. Truett "Pastor," and when I came so much younger, they called me "Pastor." I have been called "pastor" ever since.

Episkopos refers to the rulership of the church. Several times does the apostle Paul refer to the pastor as the ruler of the church. Anytime there is anyone else who is leading the church, they will be a poorly-led congregation. I do not care who he is, how many there are, or however they may be organized. The church may be run by a clique, or by an organized group, or just by anybody, but God intends for the rulership of the church to lie in the pastor. He is under God, responsible to the Lord for the church. These who stand by his side are fellow helpers. A deacon is a *diakonos,* "a servant," "a helper." He is to stand by the side of the pastor and hold up his arms like Hur and Aaron. You will have a mighty church if you have laymen and deacons who stand by the side of the pastor and help him build up the house of God. They make an unbeatable team, a consecrated deacon and a dedicated pastor. It takes both of them.

The other ordained officer in the church is the *diakonos,* the "servant," the "deacon," the "layman." What a mighty contribution does that deacon have to offer to God concerning the faithfulness and dedication to the assignment to which God has called him and for which the people laid hands upon his head! The American poet, Edgar A. Guest, truly said in "The Layman":

> Leave it to the ministers,
>   And soon the church will die;
> Leave it to the women folk;
>   The young will pass it by.
>
> For the church is all that lifts us
>   From the coarse and selfish mob,
> But the church that is to prosper
>   Needs the layman on the job.
>
> Now, a layman has his business,
>   And a layman has his joys;

But he also has the training
    Of his little girls and boys.

And I wonder how he'd like it
    If there were no churches here
And he had to raise his children
    In a godless atmosphere.

When you see a church that's empty,
    Though its doors are open wide,
It is not the church that's dying;
    It's the laymen who have died;

For it's not by song or sermon
    That the church's work is done;
It's the laymen of the country
    Who for God must carry on.

In a great convocation in Washington, D.C., I heard James L. Kraft, founder of the great Kraft Food Corporation say, "I had rather be a layman in the North Shore Baptist Church in Chicago than to head the greatest corporation in America." Then he paused and added, "My first job is serving Jesus." That is an unbeatable team, a dedicated and consecrated pastor who loves his people and is responsible to God for their souls, and a dedicated layman, a dedicated laywoman standing by his side, serving the Lord in humility, in faithfulness, and in deepest consecration.

The Destiny of the Church Is Two-fold

The destiny of the church, the assignment of the church is two-fold. First, we have the tremendous commission from our Lord to do a two-fold work. We are to evangelize, and we are to teach the mind of God that is in Christ

Jesus. The missionary impact of the church upon the world is the greatest single phenomenon in human history. That is our assignment as a congregation of the Lord. We are to mediate the truth of God. We are to do it in our Jerusalem, our home town. We are to do it in our Samaria, in all of America. We are to do it unto the uttermost parts of the earth. The evangelization of the world, the winning of people to Christ is our heavenly mandate.

Second, we are to be ready and prepared for the Lord Jesus when he comes. We are to have a people watching and waiting for the Lord when he descends in glory and in power from the sky. I think that is the whole doctrine of election. Election is that God has promised if Jesus dies, there will be a people who will trust in his name and who will be waiting for him when he comes. His death will not be in vain, it will not be barren, sterile, or fruitless. That is the great destiny and assignment of the church which itself is a *musterion,* and when he comes we shall be raptured away, we shall be caught away, we shall be lifted up to meet our Lord in the air. This is our vast and endless assignment, loving Jesus in life, loving Jesus in age, loving Jesus in death, and praising Jesus through all eternity. Our church is built around the blessed Jesus, our prayers are offered in the name of Jesus, our preaching is centered in the glorious gospel of the precious Savior, and our songs and praises lift up glory his wonderful name, that our children be brought up in the love and nurture of the precious Savior, and that our whole lives be cemented together in hope, charity, and faith in the blessed Jesus, our all in all.

> I entered once a home of care,
>   And penury and want were there,
> But joy and peace withal.

I asked the aged mother whence
Her helpless widowhood's defense,
    She answered, "Christ is all."

I saw the martyr at the stake,
    The flames could not his courage shake,
Nor death his soul appal,
    I asked him whence his strength was given,
He looked triumphantly to heaven and answered,
    "Christ is all."

I stood beside the dying bed,
    Where lay a child with aching head,
Waiting Jesus' call.
    I saw him smile, t'was sweet as May,
And as his spirit passed away,
    He whispered, "Christ is all."

I dreamed that hoary time had fled,
    The earth and sea gave up their dead,
A fire dissolved this ball.
    I saw the church's ransomed throng,
I caught the burden of their song,
    T'was this, that Christ is all in all.

Our heavenly assignment and mandate is to praise the Lord, to speak of the Lord, to pray to the Lord Jesus, to gather together in the name of the Lord Jesus, reading and learning about the Lord Jesus, preaching the gospel of the Lord Jesus, making appeal in the name of the blessed Jesus, waiting for the Lord Jesus from heaven, and some day in the presence of God's assembled redeemed, we will look upon his face, rejoicing in his presence, and lending our souls and voices and hearts and lives to the exaltation and praise of the blessed Savior, world without end. Amen!

12.
Christ, the Word of God

In the beginning was the Word, and the Word was with God, and the Word was God.

The same was in the beginning with God.

All things were made by him; and without him was not any thing made that was made (John 1:1–3).

As a background, let us read some Scripture passages which will describe to us the person of Jesus our Lord.

God, who at sundry times and in divers manners spake in time past unto the fathers by the prophets,

Hath in these last days spoken unto us by his Son, whom he hath appointed heir of all things, by whom also he made the worlds;

Who being the brightness of his glory, and the express image of his person, and upholding all things by the word of his power, when he had by himself purged our sins, sat down on the right hand of the Majesty on high;

Being made so much better than the angels, as he hath by inheritance obtained a more excellent name than they (Heb. 1:1–4).

And I saw heaven opened, and behold a white horse; and he that sat upon him was called Faithful and True, and in righteousness he doth judge and make war.

His eyes were as a flame of fire, and on his head were many crowns; and he had a name written, that no man knew, but he himself.

And he was clothed with a vesture dipped in blood: and his name is called The Word of God (Rev. 19:11–13).

To Love the Word Is to Love God

The written word, the spoken word, the incarnate word are all three inseparably tied together. God is identified with his Word and the Word is identified with God— the written Word, the spoken Word, and the incarnate Word. Whenever I receive the Word of God, I receive God himself. When I believe the Word of God, I believe God himself. Spiritually, when I know the Word of God, I know God himself. When I trust the Word of God, I trust God himself. God and his Word are identified forever. The Psalmist says, "For ever, O Lord, thy word is settled in heaven" (Ps. 119:89). God's Word is like God himself, the same yesterday, today, and forever.

The Universe Is Upheld by the Word of God

The whole universe is upheld by the Word of God as evidenced in Hebrews 1:3, "upholding all things by the word of his power." When we look into this vast creation, what hand is it that guides these planets in their orbits, and what omnipotence is it which guides the destiny of our created universe? It is the almighty hand of the omnipotent God upholding all things by the Word of his power.

One time I stood on the shores of the Indian Ocean. It seemed to me that I was standing straight up and the great body of water was held in the arms of the sea. Not long after that I was standing on the shores of the Gulf of Mexico, and again, it seemed that I was standing straight up and that the great Gulf was held in the arms of the sea.

I then looked at a globe. On the globe one of the seas appears to be upside down. They are diametrically opposite from each other. If I was standing upright on the shores of the Indian Ocean, then I was standing on my head on the shores of the Gulf of Mexico. If I was standing straight up on the shores of Mexico, then I was standing head down on the shore of the Indian Ocean. That poses a problem for which anybody would ask an answer. If the oceans are on opposite sides and one of them is upside down, why does not the water spill out? Why do not the people who live around the Indian Ocean fall off of this planet? What holds them to it? What holds this universe together? That is a logical question, and we take it to a learned scientist. He knows everything.

We say to the learned and scholarly scientist: "Scientist, we want you to look at the globe. If the Gulf of Mexico is on top, then the Indian Ocean is down below. If the Indian Ocean is on top, then the Gulf of Mexico is down below. What we want to know is, if the Indian Ocean is down below, why does not the water spill out? What holds this universe together? Why do not the people fall off of the globe?"

He says to me, "Why, you idiot. Do not you know why those people do not fall off, why that water does not spill out, and do not you know what holds this universe together? Gravity. Gravity is what holds the oceans in their basins, and gravity is what holds this universe together."

I smile at my ignorance and say, "Why in the world

did not I think of that? Certainly, gravity is what holds this world together. That is why the oceans do not spill out; that is why the people do not fly off of the planet. They are held here together by gravity." Then I just happen to think, "Well, Mr. Scientist" (who knows all the answers), "What is gravity?"

He says, "Why you stupid moron, do not you know what gravity is? Gravity is what holds the world together!"

How lucid and how learned! Gravity is what holds the world together and what holds the world together is gravity.

I hold my Bible in my hand, I drop it, and it falls down. Why does it not fall up? Why does it not fall out? Why does it not fall off? Nobody knows. Nobody who ever lived knows. One cannot explain it, just as one cannot explain anything. One just observes, that is all. It is God's mystery of creation. Because scientists do not know, they invent a word and say that "gravity" is the reason that things fall down and not up, out, or off. "Upholding all things by the word of his power"— it is God who holds this universe together.

We Are Convicted by the Word of God

We are convicted by the Word of God. Let us read the Scripture again:

> The word of God is quick, and powerful, and sharper than any two-edged sword, piercing even to the dividing asunder of soul and spirit, and of the joints and marrow, and is a discerner of the thoughts and intents of the heart. . . . But all things are naked and opened unto the eyes of him with whom we have to do (Heb. 4:12–13).

We are convicted by the penetrating sharpness and quickness of the Word of God.

We Are Born Again by the Word of God

We are saved; we are born again by the Word of God. We continue reading from God's Word:

> Being born again, not of corruptible seed, but of incorruptible, by the word of God, which liveth and abideth for ever. . . . And this is the word which by the gospel is preached unto you (1 Pet. 1:23–25).
>
> Of his own will begat he us with the word of truth (Jas. 1:18).
>
> Now ye are clean through the word which I have spoken unto you (John 15:3).
>
> That he might sanctify and cleanse it with the washing of water by the word (Eph. 5:26).

That is the interpretation of our Lord's words in John 3:5: "Except a man be born of water and of the Spirit, he cannot enter into the kingdom of God." That is, except a man be born of the Word, the cleansing of the Word, and the regenerating power of the Spirit of God, he cannot be saved. No man is ever saved apart from the preaching, the believing, and the receiving of the testimony of the Word of God through Christ our Lord. We are saved by and through the acceptance of the Word of God.

We Are Kept from Sin by the Word of God

The Bible tells us that we are kept from sin by the Word of God. We read again: "Thy word have I hid in mine heart, that I might not sin against thee" (Ps. 119:11).

We Are to Walk by the Word of God

There is a beautiful verse in the Psalm that describes for us how the Christian is to walk. "Thy word is a lamp unto my feet, and a light unto my path" (Ps. 119:105).

We Are to Live by the Word of God

Our Lord Jesus quoted from Deuteronomy when he said: "Man shall not live by bread alone, but by every word that proceedeth out of the mouth of God" (Matt. 4:4).

It is an amazing report that when the Lord answered the tempter in the trial in the wilderness, every trial he answered with and by the Word of the living God.

We Are to Die by the Word of God

"Because thou hast kept the word of my patience, I also will keep thee from the hour of temptation, which shall come upon all the world" (Rev. 3:10).

There was a beautiful woman in our church who fell in love with and married a man from a faraway state. They chose to come to Dallas to live. He was a very worldly man, for all of his life he had been a leader in a worldly assignment. She brought him to church faithfully. As the days passed, he was converted, he made a confession of his faith in the Lord, and I baptized him. It seemed as though, because of the years that he had spent in the world, that he sought to redeem the time. He was doubly faithful, doubly prayerful, and he read the Bible day and night. In the car, he would place the Bible by his side. When he went to bed at night, he had his Bible in his hand. When he shaved, he would prop up the Bible by the side of the mirror and read the Word of God. I was so grateful for him and proud of him. Then in one of those experiences that brings sorrow to your heart, suddenly without announcement, he died of a heart attack. When I went to conduct the memorial service, I stood by his wife and looked at his silent face in the casket. To my great surprise, he was holding his Bible in his hand in the casket. I turned to his wife and said: "I have never seen that before in my life. There he lies with a Bible in his hand."

She said, "When he was converted, he was given to the calling of God, redeeming the days that he had lost and misspent out in the world. When the funeral director had prepared his body and placed it in the casket, I went to his room, got his Bible, and I placed it here in his hand as the last witness and testimony to the people who will be here at the funeral service that the Bible is the true, infallible, and living Word of God." We are to die by the Word of God.

We Are to Preach the Word of God

We are to preach the Word of God. The Bible says: "All scripture is given by inspiration of God, and is profitable for doctrine, for reproof, for correction, for instruction in righteousness: That the man of God may be perfect, throughly furnished unto all good works" (2 Tim. 3:16–17).

What a shame there is a chapter heading there dividing the "therefore!" The first verse of the fourth chapter says, "I charge thee therefore." The "therefore" points back to what the apostle Paul had just said, that the Scripture is the inspired Word of God. The apostle, writing to Timothy, his son in the ministry, says, "I charge thee therefore," based on the inspiration, the infallibility, the inerrancy of the Holy Scripture, "preach the Word." We read in 2 Timothy:

> I charge thee therefore before God, and the Lord Jesus Christ, who shall judge the quick and the dead at his appearing and his kingdom;
> Preach the word; be instant in season, out of season; reprove, rebuke, exhort with all longsuffering and doctrine (2 Tim. 4:1–2).

How does one get people to God? How does one win souls for Christ? Paul says that it is by preaching the Word of God. That is what the preacher is to do. He is not to stand in the pulpit and say, "Thus saith Einstein" or "Thus saith Dr. Sounding Brass" or "Thus saith Professor Dry-as-Dust." What he is to do is to stand in the pulpit with a Bible in his hand and say, "Thus saith the Lord God." When he does that, people are fed; they are nourished; and they grow in grace and in the knowledge of the Lord.

We can read in the newspaper on every editorial page; we can buy a magazine at a newsstand and read it; we can listen to the commentaries on the radio and television. The commentators are always talking about the issues that are sweeping over this world—economics, politics, war and peace, race, and a thousand other events. What we want to know when we come to church is not the rehashing of what we have been listening to and reading every day of the week. What we want to know is does God say anything? We know what the Secretary of State says. We know what the President says. We know what all the people are saying. What we want to know is: "Does God say anything? Preacher, tell us."

I remember a scene between the king, Zedekiah, and the prophet Jeremiah. Zedekiah asked the prophet of God, "Is there any word from the Lord in the trials we face?" In inexorable death that is coming, is there any word from the Lord? Does God say anything? Jeremiah answered, "He does. God has a word to say." God always speaks to us. He speaks to the occasion, to the trial, to the trouble, to the tribulation, to the open doors, to the opportunities, and to all of the other vicissitudes, fortunes, and circumstances of life. God talks; God speaks; and he speaks to us in his living Word.

Our Assurance of Heaven Is the Word and Promise of God

Our assurance of heaven is the Word and the promise of the Lord. The Bible confirms: "Verily, verily, I say unto you, He that heareth my word, and believeth on him that sent me, hath everlasting life, and shall not come into condemnation; but is passed from death unto life" (John 5:24).

I was converted when I was a child ten years old. In the little town in which I grew up, we were having a revival meeting in the white, cracker box of a church house in which we called upon the name of the Lord. There was a visiting pastor from Dalhart who was holding the revival services. He stayed at our house during the days of the revival meeting. Every night after the service was over, my mother would seat him at a kitchen table and pour for him a glass of home-churned buttermilk. I sat by the preacher's side at the kitchen table. While he drank his glass of buttermilk, he would talk to me about the Lord. On a weekday morning, I received permission from my parents to be dismissed from school to attend the ten o'clock morning service. That morning when I walked into our little church, I happened to be seated in the pew behind my sainted mother. When the preacher had finished his sermon, he made the appeal. The people stood up and were singing, "There Is a Fountain Filled with Blood." My mother, who was crying, turned to me and said, "Son, today will you take Jesus as your Savior?"

I answered: "Mother, yes. Today, this minute, now, I will take the Lord Jesus as my Savior." I went forward and gave the pastor my hand in token of the fact that I had received the Lord Jesus into my heart as my Savior.

I began to preach when I was seventeen years of age. For the first ten years, I preached out in the country and in small villages. For the first several of those years, I preached in a country place where there was no store, there was no highway, there was no anything. The little church was located on the side of a creek. We had by the side of the church a tabernacle. In the summertime we had the most marvelous of all the revival meetings that one could have ever attended. They were called "camp meetings." The people came and camped on the ground all ten days of the revival. That is where I began preaching in the summertime—outdoors under tabernacles, under arbors.

In those days they had what was called grove prayer meetings. The women usually would stay under the tabernacle and have their prayer service. The men would go to a grove, that is, under the shade of the trees, and there they would gather for their prayer service. Then the men and women would come together under the tabernacle, and I would preach. That is the way I began my ministry under those tabernacles.

In those grove prayer meetings, the men would give their testimony. I never heard such testimonies in my life. They were marvelous. They were apostolic. They were Pauline.

A typical example was when one of the men pointed to a place and said: "I had been under the heavy burden of my sin for years, and I was standing in that place right there. While I stood there, suddenly there came down from God a ball of fire from heaven. It burst over my head and struck me to the ground. How long I lay in that state, I do not know, but when I came to myself and stood up, the heavy burden of my sin rolled away." Then he described the new life and the new day, how the mules looked different when he plowed, how the birds sang, how the trees flowered, and how the sky looked.

But the testimonies of the men had an effect upon me beyond what one would have thought. I never saw a ball of fire. I never saw an angel from heaven. I never saw a ray of light from glory. I was converted as a boy ten years of age, just trusting the Lord Jesus as my Savior. I came to the conclusion that I was not converted, that I did not know the Lord, that I was not a Christian, that I was not regenerated, that I was not saved.

You cannot conceive of the turmoil, the trouble, and the battle in my heart. For years—not a day, not a month, but for years—after I would stand every Sunday before my little country congregation and preach, every night I would get down by my bed and cry unto the Lord: "Lord, I am not really saved. I am not really regenerated. I have not been saved. Lord, I am not a Christian. I have not had a wonderful experience that I can tell the people about. I have not seen an angel. I have not seen a ball of fire. I have not seen a light from heaven. Lord, I am not saved."

That went on for years. As I knelt before God, I cried

to God for a great sign from glory that I was regenerated, that I was a Christian, that I was saved. "Lord, Lord, open the doors of glory. Let me see a light. Send an angel, Lord, that I can have a mighty experience to tell the people when I give my personal testimony!"

In those days, of course, I read the Bible. I read in 2 Corinthians 11 that the devil transforms himself into an angel of light. I also read in Revelation 13 that the Antichrist, the deceiver, sends fire down from heaven to deceive the people upon the earth. Then as the days passed, the truth of God finally came to my heart.

When we shall stand in the presence of the great Lord God Almighty at the judgment day of God, when the Lord's saints are entering in, and I assay to join their number, and the Lord God stops me and says, "By what right and by what prerogative do you walk on my golden streets and mingle with my redeemed?"

I will say to him: "Lord, I know that I am a Christian. I know I have been saved. I know I have been regenerated. I saw an angel from heaven. I know I have been saved and I am a Christian. I saw an angel from heaven."

Satan will laugh: "Ha, ha, ha! He saw an angel from heaven! I was that angel. I transformed myself into an angel of light just to deceive him," and he will proceed to drag my soul down to hell. What could I say? What would I do?

Or in the final day when I stand in the great assize before the judgment bar of Almighty God, when God's saints are entering in, when the Lord God stops me and says, "By what right and by what authority do you enter my beautiful city, walk on my golden streets, pass through my gates of pearl, and mingle with my redeemed?"

I shall reply: "Lord God, you know I am saved. I have

been regenerated. I am a Christian. I saw a ball of fire
fall over my head and it struck me to the ground. I know
I have been saved. Lord, I saw a ball of fire."

Satan will laugh: "Ha, ha, ha! He saw a ball of fire. I
sent that ball of fire from heaven just to deceive him."
What could I say and what could I do as he drags my
soul down to hell?

Then the truth came to my heart. Someday when I
stand at the judgment seat of Christ, when God's people
are entering in, that throng of saved and blood-bought
people, and I assay to join their number, when the Lord
God stops me and says, "By what right and by what
prerogative do you join my redeemed and enter my beautiful city?"

I then will say to the Lord: "Dear God, when I was
a boy ten years old, they were having a revival meeting
in the little church in which I grew up in the small town.
The preacher stayed in our home. Every night after he
preached, as he drank a glass of buttermilk, he talked
to me about you. On a weekday ten-o'clock-morning-
hour when I went to church, I happened to be seated
back of my mother. She turned to me and said, 'Son,
today, will you take Jesus as your Savior?' I said, 'Mother,
today I will take Jesus as my Savior.' Lord Jesus, you
said here in your Book, 'He came unto his own and his
own received him not, but as many as received him, to
them gave he the right, the authority, the prerogative,
the power to become the children of God, even to them
that trust, that believe in his name.' Lord God, I am just
depending upon you to keep your word. That is all, just
trusting in you, Lord, to keep your word that you did
not deceive me, that you have not lied to me, that you
have not misled me. I am just trusting you, Lord, to keep
your word." Then I dare Satan to scoff, to ridicule, to

scorn, and to laugh. For you see, my salvation is not a matter between him and me. Even Michael the archangel dared not rebuke him. I am no equal for him. But my salvation does not depend upon my being mightier than Satan. My salvation is a matter of the Lord keeping his word. It is a matter between him and Satan. He said, "I will never leave thee, I will never fail thee, and I will never forsake thee."

I have never doubted my salvation since. I settled it in the presence of the Lord. I can awaken at two o'clock in the morning and there that promise is: "As many as received him, to them gave he the right to become the children of God."

If I were to see an angel, if I were to see a ball of fire, if I were to see a light from heaven, now it would never occur to me to connect it with my salvation. It would never enter my mind or my heart. If God were to give me a vision of angels, I would praise his name forever. O Lord, how wonderful to see heaven opened and to look at God's angels! I would praise his name if I were to see a vision of angels, but it would never occur to me now to make it a part of my salvation. My salvation is based not upon angels, not upon balls of fire, not upon a great experience, not upon a light from heaven, but I base my salvation upon the Word and the promise of God. If he prevails, I win. If he is victor, I am in the triumph. If he lives, I am saved by the Word and the promise of the crucified One!

13.
The Coming King

Pilate therefore said unto him, Art thou a king then? Jesus answered. Thou sayest that I am a king. To this end was I born, and for this cause came I into the world, that I should bear witness unto the truth. Every one that is of the truth heareth my voice (John 18:37).

In the story of John 18, Pilate is looking at the despised figure of Christ with a crown of thorns on his head, a purple robe over his shoulder, and a reed for a scepter in his hand. He is bloody and beaten by the scourging of the Roman legions. Pilate says unbelievingly, "Art thou, you, a king?" Jesus answered in the most emphatic way that the Greek language can express it, to repeat the question. "Thou sayest that I am a king. To this end was I born, and for this cause came I into the world" (John 18:37). Jesus is King.

In an unconditional covenant, the Lord God promised the land of Palestine to Abraham and to the seed of Israel forever. We read in Psalm 105:

> He hath remembered his covenant for ever, the word which he commanded to a thousand generations. Which covenant he made with Abraham, and his oath unto Isaac;
> And confirmed the same unto Jacob for a law, and to Israel for an everlasting covenant:

Saying, Unto thee will I give the land of Canaan,
the lot of your inheritance (vv. 8–11).

The rest of the world is for all the others, but the
land of Canaan, the land of Palestine, belongs to the
seed of Israel. It was promised to Abraham, to Isaac, and
to Jacob by an unconditional covenant forever.

The same Lord God said to David that he should have
a son who would sit upon his throne, world without
end. The Lord said to David in 2 Samuel:

When thy days be fulfilled, and thou shalt sleep
with thy fathers, I will set up thy seed after thee,
which shall proceed out of thy bowels, and I will
establish his kingdom.
And thine house and thy kingdom shall be established for ever before thee: thy throne shall be established for ever. (7:12,16).

The same Lord God who promised to Abraham, Isaac,
and Jacob that the lot of their inheritance forever should
be the land of Canaan is the same Lord God who promised
to David that he should have a son who would reign
over the house of Israel forever.

The prophet Isaiah described that glorious Son and
that mighty King in the seed and line of David. He said
in Isaiah 9:

Nevertheless the dimness shall not be such as was
in her vexation, when at the first he lightly afflicted
the land of Zebulun and the land of Naphtali, and
afterward did more grievously afflict her by the way
of the sea, beyond Jordan, in Galilee of the nations.
The people that walked in darkness have seen a

great light: they that dwell in the land of the shadow
of death, upon them hath the light shined. . . .

For unto us a child is born, unto us a son is given:
and the government shall be upon his shoulder: and
his name shall be called Wonderful, Counsellor, The
mighty God, The everlasting Father, The Prince of
Peace.

Of the increase of his government and peace there
shall be no end, upon the throne of David, and upon
his kingdom, to order it, and to establish it with
judgment and with justice from henceforth even for
ever. The zeal of the Lord of hosts will perform
this (vv. 1–2,6–7).

Seven hundred fifty years after that prophecy, the angel
Gabriel was sent to a little village in Galilee named Nazareth, to a virgin Jewess named Mary, and announced
to her that she should be the mother of this foretold,
foreordained child. We follow the story in Luke 1:

The angel said unto her, Fear not, Mary: for thou
hast found favour with God.

And, behold, thou shalt conceive in thy womb,
and bring forth a son, and shalt call his name Jesus.

He shall be great, and shall be called the Son of
the Highest: and the Lord God shall give unto him
the throne of his father David:

And he shall reign over the house of Jacob for
ever; and of his kingdom there shall be no end.

Then said Mary unto the angel, How shall this
be, seeing I know not a man?

And the angel answered and said unto her, The
Holy Ghost shall come upon thee, and the power
of the Highest shall overshadow thee: therefore also

that holy thing which shall be born of thee shall be called the Son of God (vv. 30–35).

Upon a night of nights, when the heavens were radiant with the glory of God, when the very air was resonant with the rhythm of infinite harmonies, when each star seemed to be lowered like a golden lamp earthward with invisible hands, the Child was born. An angel suddenly descended from heaven and announced to the startled shepherds in Bethlehem that the Savior of the world had come. Upon that announcement, the heavens parted like a scroll, and the angel chorus, waiting from the dawn of creation, flung upward their paean of praise, "Glory to God in the highest," and then flung downward their benedictory blessing, "and on earth peace, good will toward men." The covenant King had come!

In the fifteenth year of Tiberias Caesar, Jesus, who was about thirty years of age, was baptized by John the Baptist in the Jordan River. The Lord immediately went forth to declare the coming of the covenant kingdom and to present himself as the promised and covenant King. He carried with him the credentials of his royalty and his kingship. Through his mother Mary, he was descended from David through the line of Nathan. Through the husband of Mary, Joseph, he was descended from David through the line of Solomon. Both by legal right and by blood inheritance, Jesus was a King.

He carried with him also the credentials of a beautiful and sinless life. He bore also the credentials of wonderful words: "Never a man spake like that man." He also carried the credentials of wondrous works: "It was never so seen in Israel." Upon a day at the exact time foretold by Gabriel to Daniel the prophet-statesman, in the exact manner as prophesied by Zechariah, the Lord Jesus Christ, the covenant King, came into Zion, lowly and riding upon the foal of a donkey, to present himself as the covenant King, the Prince of Peace. As he came into the holy city of Jerusalem, the people shouted with inexpressible exultation and delight: "Hosanna in the highest! Blessed is he that cometh in the name of the Lord! Hosanna to the Son of David!" When the scribes and the Pharisees sought to still those who were so crying, the Lord replied: "If these should hold their peace, the stones would immediately cry out" (Luke 19:40).

It was the great covenant day in the life of the chosen people of God. It was the great consummating moment of all history. The covenant King had come, Jesus, King of the Jews.

He Is a Rejected King

Jesus is a rejected King. The Lord stood on the witness stand in the Sanhedrin, the highest court of Israel. Before him stands the high priest who presides over the Sanhedrin. The high priest says to the Lord in Matthew 26:

> The high priest answered and said unto him, I adjure thee by the living God, that thou tell us whether thou be the Christ, the Son of God.
> Jesus saith unto him, Thou hast said: nevertheless I say unto you, Hereafter shall ye see the Son of man sitting on the right hand of power, and coming in the clouds of heaven (vv. 63–64).

When the Lord said that under oath, the high priest rent his garments and turned to the other seventy of the Sanhedrin and said: "You have heard his blasphemy. What do you say?"

They cried, saying, "Crucify him, crucify him!"

At that time capital punishment had been taken out of the hands of the Sanhedrin and of the Jewish state, and it was invested in the court of the Roman procurator. The Jews, therefore, took the Lord Jesus to Pontius Pilate and accused him of sedition, saying, "He says he is a King." The Lord was standing there, so humble, so patient, so quiet.

Pilate said, "He? A King?"

"Yes, he says he is Christ, a King. He is guilty of treason and sedition."

Pilate said, "I will scourge him and let him go."

So the Roman legions beat him, and in contempt both for the Jew and for this lowly Nazarene, crowned him with thorns, put a cast-off, purple robe over his shoulder, put a stick in his hand for a scepter, and mockingly, scornfully bowed the knee, saying, "Hail, King of the Jews."

Pilate, seeing the Lord so bloodied now with the awesome scourging, such a ridiculous figure with a crown made out of thorns and a dirty, ragged, cast-off robe, and with a reed in his hand, brought him forth and said, "Behold your King!"

They answered, saying: "We have no king but Caesar. Crucify him!"

Pontius Pilate, the procurator, delivered him into the hands of four quaternions of soldiers who took him to Calvary and raised him between earth and sky and crucified him. But above his head Pilate wrote the superscription of his accusation, "This Is Jesus, a King."

The scribes and the Pharisees went to the procurator and said, "Do not write 'This Is Jesus the King.' Write 'This Is Jesus Who Said He Is a King.' "

Pilate replied that famous reply, *"Gegrapha, gegrapha,"* "What I have written, I have written." Jesus was crucified

a King, and he died a King. The superscription was written in Greek, in Hebrew, and in Latin for the whole
world to know. Jesus died a King, a rejected King. "He
came unto his own, and his own received him not" (John
1:11).

He Is an Exiled King

He is an exiled King. In Luke 19 our Lord says, speaking
of himself: "A certain nobleman went into a far country
to receive for himself a kingdom, and to return. And
he called his ten servants, and delivered them ten pounds,
and said unto them, Occupy till I come" (vv. 12–13).

The nobleman went away into the far country and
left his servants here to work in his name. The Lord
Jesus, King Jesus, went away into another country, up
there into heaven, and sat down at the right hand of
the majesty on high, waiting for the consummation. He
is an exiled King waiting in heaven until the appointed
time to come again.

The Great Intermission and the Vast Interlude

When Jesus died on the cross, how Satan must have
exulted! How he must have rejoiced! "Look, look, Jesus
is dead! Israel has crucified her own firstborn son. Jesus
is dead. Look, the chosen family and the chosen race
are in unbelief. They have rejected their King!" I can
hear Satan cry in exultation and rejoicing: "All of the
promises of God have come to nought. Every prophecy
is fallen to the ground. Sin shall reign forever! Darkness
shall reign forever! Death shall reign forever!" I can hear
Satan rejoice through the scribe, the Pharisee, and the
Sadducee. He marches up and down in front of Jesus
as he dies on the cross.

But Satan did not know. It was a secret kept in the

heart of God that there should be between the sixty-ninth and the seventieth weeks of Daniel an interlude, an intermission, (a *musterion,* Paul calls it in Ephesians 3), between his coming to the cross and between his second coming with a crown. There should be an intermission, the age of grace, the age of the Holy Spirit in which God would call out of the whole world a people for his own. They should be called *ekklesia,* "the called-out ones," in our language, "the church."

The gospel of salvation, redemption, and invitation should be preached to all men everywhere. Wherever there is a man who would turn and believe, he also should be added to the family of God. There would be one household of faith with Jew and Gentile, Greek and barbarian, Roman and provincial, black and white, male and female, learned and unlearned, rich and poor, all alike precious in the sight of God, belonging to the redeemed family of the Lord.

This intermission, this full interlude, this age of grace, this age of the Holy Spirit, this age of the calling out is this present age when God is fashioning a new body, a new creation called the church, the bride of Christ.

But what of the kingdom? Is there to be no kingdom? Has God forgotten the kingdom? You see, Jesus is the head of the church. He is not the "king" of the church. There is no such wordage in the Bible. Jesus is a King over a kingdom and what of the kingdom? Will the kingdom ever come? Will Jesus ever reign as King over the earth? The disciples asked him that question in Acts 1 as he began to ascend into heaven: "Lord, wilt thou at this time restore again the kingdom to Israel?" (v. 6).

What a propitious moment, what an advantageous hour for the Lord to answer the disciples, saying: "There is not going to be any kingdom. There will never be a kingdom. I am not a King. It will never be." He did not say that. When they asked him, "Lord, wilt thou at this time restore the Kingdom?" the Lord replied: "It is not for you to know the times or the seasons which the Lord hath kept in his own hands. But you preach the gospel, fill the church, sound out the call, gather the redeemed into the family of God. The kingdom is postponed, but it will come some glorious, triumphant, consummating day; the kingdom will come."

Jesus Is a Coming King

He is coming under a two-fold simile. He is coming first as a thief in the night, and he is coming second as the livid lightning splits the bosom of the sky and shines from the east to the west. So shall the Lord come in the *parousia,* the great revelation, the *apokalupsis* of the reigning King.

First, he is coming under the imagery of a thief in the night. He is coming unannounced, suddenly, with unsandaled feet, quietly, furtively, clandestinely, secretly. He is coming as a thief to steal away his jewels, to take out of the world his pearl of price and his treasure hid in a field. He is coming as a thief to rapture away his people, and it will include us all. We all shall be changed. We, who are alive and remain unto the coming of the Lord when he comes as a thief in the night shall be suddenly raptured away to meet our Lord in the air.

Those who have fallen asleep in Jesus will rise first. The trumpet shall sound, the archangel shall speak, and these who have fallen asleep in Jesus will rise first. Then all of us shall be changed, caught up to meet our Lord in the air. There shall not be a bone left in the region of death, not a relic for the devil to gloat over. We shall

all be raised, and we shall all be changed. We shall all be caught up to meet our Lord in the air.

As it was in the days of Enoch, just suddenly he was gone. As it was in the days of Noah, the Lord shut him away in the ark. As it was in the days of Lot and the angel took him out before the judgments of the Almighty fell upon the earth, thus the Lord shall come, furtively, secretly, as a thief in the night, to rapture away his people before the judgments of the great tribulation.

Then he shall come openly, and every eye shall see him, the *parousia,* the *apokalupsis.* As the lightning shines in the heavens above, so the glory of the presence of the Lord shall be seen. The text of the apocalypse of the revelation is Revelation 1:7, "Behold, he cometh with clouds; and every eye shall see him." As the brother of the Lord, Jude says, "Behold, the Lord cometh with ten thousands of his saints" (Jude 14).

The Lord is coming with his people, descending from heaven, and he is coming in glory. He is coming in the glory of God as God the Son and the Son of God. He is coming in the glory of the angels as the captain of the host of heaven. He is coming in the glory of the church as the bridegroom with the bride. He is coming in his own glory as the Son of God, as the Son of Abraham, as the Son of David, as the Son of Man.

He is coming in his own glory as the virgin-born man, the crucified man, the risen man, the God-man, the manifest and eternal Son of the highest. He is coming as the King of the Jews. He is coming as the King of the nations. He is coming as the King of kings. He is coming as the Lord God *pantokrator,* the Almighty God himself. He is coming as the re-Creator and the restorer of this earth. He is coming to be Lord and King over all creation.

Then shall be brought to pass all of the sayings in

the prophecies, such as Micah: "They shall beat their swords into plowshares, and their spears into pruning-hooks: nation shall not lift up a sword against nation, neither shall they learn war any more" (Micah 4:3).

The Prince of Peace has come. Then shall be brought to pass the beautiful prophecy of Isaiah:

> The wolf also shall dwell with the lamb, and the leopard shall lie down with the kid; and the calf and the young lion and the fatling together; and a little child shall lead them.
>
> And the cow and the bear shall feed; their young ones shall lie down together: and the lion shall eat straw like the ox.
>
> And the sucking child shall play on the hole of the asp, and the weaned child shall put his hand on the cockatrice's den.
>
> They shall not hurt nor destroy in all my holy mountain: for the earth shall be full of the knowledge of the Lord, as the waters cover the sea (11:6–9).

The thought of the imminent return of our Lord has two repercussions in the human heart. One is terror. If my heart is in this world and if my life is given to vanity and to sin, the thought of the coming of Christ terrifies me, even as it is described in the sixth chapter of Revelation:

> And said to the mountains and rocks, Fall on us, and hide us from the face of him that sitteth on the throne, and from the wrath of the Lamb: For the great day of his wrath is come: and who shall be able to stand? (vv. 16–17).

To these who reject our Lord and live in sin and compromise, the coming of Christ is a terror. But to those who love the Lord Jesus, the thought of the appearance of our Savior is of all things sweet, dear, and precious, even as the apostle John replied when the Lord closed the Apocalypse with the word: "He which testifieth these things saith, Surely I come quickly" (Rev. 22:20). The sainted apostle replied, "Amen. Even so, come, Lord Jesus" (v. 20).

> It may be at midday, it may be at twilight,
> It may be per chance that the blackness of night
> Will burst into light in the blaze of His glory,
> When Jesus comes for His own.
>
> O joy, O delight, should I go without dying,
> No sickness, no sadness, no dread, and no crying,
> Caught up through the clouds with our Lord into
>   glory,
> When Jesus comes for His own.
>
> O Lord Jesus, how long, how long,
> E'er we shout the glad song.
> Christ returneth, Christ returneth.
> Hallelujah, Amen.

Welcome, King, Lord, Savior, the blessed Jesus!

14.

The Whosoever Wills

The Spirit and the bride say, Come. And let him that heareth say, Come. And let him that is athirst come. And whosoever will, let him take the water of life freely" (Rev. 22:17).

This text concerns the last invitation in the Word of God. "And whosoever will, *ho thelon,* let him take the water of life freely." This is a magnificent text, a gloriously incomparable invitation. The Spirit of God pleads with a man to come to Jesus. The bride of Christ, the church of the living Lord, pleads with a man to come to Jesus. No one is happier or more thankful in the earth than the church when someone comes down the aisle to give himself to Jesus. "Let him that heareth say, Come." Let the stranger, the sojourner, and the passerby repeat the glad refrain, "Come, come to Jesus." "And let him that is athirst come." Our Lord said that whosoever drinks of the water of this life shall thirst again. But if you would have life to the full, God's abounding invitation is that whosoever will, let him take the water of happiness freely.

God Seeks to Save Adam's Children

You see, God had done everything that even God could do to save the evil, wicked, and obstreperous children of old man Adam. When the Lord God placed our first parents in the Garden of Eden, he said, "Of every tree in the garden you may freely eat; just one I reserve for myself."

Our first parents said, "No, we want it all." They took every tree in the garden and died.

The Lord God looked down from heaven at the progeny of old man Adam and said, "Thus will I do that they might live." He wrote his Ten Commandments on tables of stone and handed them to the children of Adam and said, "Do this and thou shalt live."

The children of old man Adam said, "No, we will not do this." They broke every one of the commandments of the Lord God.

The Lord God looked down from heaven on the evil children of old man Adam and said, "Thus I will do that they might be saved. I will send them my prophets."

The prophets came and preached, saying, "Turn ye, turn ye to the Lord, for why will ye die?"

The children of old man Adam replied, "No, we will not turn to the Lord." They took God's prophets and slew them, fed them to the lions, and threw them into fiery furnaces.

The Lord God looked down from heaven and said, "Thus will I do to save the children of old man Adam. I will send a forerunner to announce the coming of the kingdom of God."

The great Baptist preacher came and said, "Prepare ye the way of the Lord."

The children of old man Adam said, "No, we will not prepare the way of the Lord." They took God's forerunner and cut off his head, and he died in his own blood.

The Lord God looked down from heaven on the children of old man Adam and said, "Thus will I do that they might be saved. They will reverence my Son." So God sent his only begotten Son into the world, but the children of old man Adam seized the Lord, took him outside of their city, nailed him to a tree, and he died like a criminal, a felon, a malefactor.

The Lord God looked down from heaven and said: "Thus will I do to save the children of old man Adam. I will raise up apostles who will preach the gospel, and the people will turn and be saved."

The apostles came and preached, saying, "If thou shalt confess with thy mouth Jesus as Lord, and believe in thine heart that he lives, thou shalt be saved."

The children of old man Adam said, "No, we will not confess with our mouths, neither will we believe in our hearts." They took God's apostles and some of them they cut off their heads with the sword, some of them they stoned to death, and others they exiled to lonely islands to die of exposure and privation.

It was then that the Lord God looked down from heaven on the wicked and iniquitous children of old man Adam and said: "I will make one other and final invitation. If a man is just willing, I will save him." *Ho thelon,* "Whosoever will, let him come."

Just a Willingness Saves a Man

The Holy Spirit said to the apostle John, "When you write this last invitation, do not write, *Ho ginoskon,* 'Whosoever understandeth,' let him come. Do not write *Ho lambano,* 'Whosoever receiveth,' let him come. Do not write, *Ho paschon,* 'Whosoever feeleth,' let him come. Do not write *Ho pistuon,* 'Whosoever loveth,' let him come. But John, in this last invitation write, *Ho thelon,* 'Whosoever will.' If a man is just willing, let him come, and I will forgive his sins, I will write his name in the Book of Life, and I will save him forever." What an amazing invitation!

It is like this. When I was a teenager, preaching out under open tabernacles and arbors, on a Saturday night in West Texas I poured my heart as zealously and prayerfully as I knew how that the people come to the Lord and be saved. When I gave the invitation, nobody responded. As I pressed the appeal, no one came forward. Finally, I turned to the singer and said, "Wait." Then I looked at the congregation and said, "If there is anyone here just willing to be saved, just come down the aisle and ask God to save you; if the Lord does not save you, I will close the Bible, I will quit the ministry, and I will never preach again." They again sang the invitation hymn and down the aisle from outside the tabernacle where he was standing came a bowlegged cowpoke with his hand extended. He came up to me and said, "Preacher, I will take you up on that proposition."

I said, "Fine." I asked everybody to kneel, and I asked the boy: "Kneel down here by my side, and I am going to pray for you. Are you willing to be saved, are you opening your heart, and will you ask God to save you?"

He said, "I will, Preacher." So we knelt together and I prayed for him: "Dear God, this boy has come down the aisle saying that he is willing to be saved. He asks God to forgive his sins and write his name in the Book of Life. Lord, come into his heart and save him now." Then I said, "William, if God has saved you, take me by the hand."

He looked back at me and said, "Preacher, there ain't nothin' happened to me yet."

I said: "Bill, I am going to pray again. You just open your heart to God."

He said: "I will, I promise you, Preacher."

So I prayed for him, "O Lord God, save this boy and save him now." I extended my hand and asked, "Bill, if God saved you, take me by the hand."

He said: "Preacher, there ain't nothin' happened to me. I am just like I was."

I said: "Bill, we are going to try one more time. You just earnestly open your heart to God."

He said: "I will. If God will just save me, I am ready."

So I poured out my heart to the Lord once more: "Lord, you know what I said. If someone would come down the aisle and ask God to save him, and if he is not saved, I will close the Book, I will quit the ministry, and I will not preach again. Lord, save this boy and save him now, please, for Jesus' sake, Amen." Then I extended my hand to him and said, "Bill, if Jesus saved you, take me by the hand."

He looked at me and said, "Preacher, there ain't nothin' happened to me. I am just like I was." We could not stay there all night long, so we had the benediction.

When I got into the little car with the family taking me up to the ranch house, they began to kid me: "Do you know what you said? You said that if anybody would come down that aisle and ask God to save him, if he was not saved, you would close your Bible, quit the ministry, and you would never preach again."

They thought that was the biggest joke they had ever heard, and they laughed and carried on. But when they found that I was just about to die, they never said another word.

When we got up to the house, I asked to be dismissed and I went into the room they had assigned for me. I put my Bible down and got down on my knees and said: "Lord, this is it for me. I never dreamed that you would turn down somebody who wanted to be saved. I never thought but that the Bible was true when it says, 'Whosoever shall call upon the name of the Lord shall be saved,' and 'whosoever will, let him come.' Lord, I do not know what to do. I said I would close the Bible, quit the ministry, and never preach again."

I went to bed and rolled and tossed all night long. I got up the next morning, prepared with the family to go to church, got in the little car, and drove down to the tabernacle grounds. When we arrived at the grounds and I opened the car door, I heard a voice up the country road hollering to me at the top of his lungs, saying, "Say, preacher, say, preacher!" There was that bowlegged cowpoke running just as fast as he could toward me. When he reached me, he put his arms around me, hugged me tight, and said, "Say, Preacher, guess what!"

I said, "What, Bill!"

He said: "Preacher, I have been saved! I have been saved!"

I said, "When were you saved?"

He said, "Last night after you prayed, on the way home, Jesus came into my heart, and I have been saved, I have been saved!"

Never in this world did I ever respond to such an experience; glad beyond any way I could describe it. When there were enough people who had arrived at the service to form a quorum, we took William into the church on confession of faith, and I baptized him in the creek by the side of the tabernacle. How happy and how glad we were that day!

When I look back over that experience, I think of how foolish it was to tempt God. I would never make a proposition like that today. Then I began thinking, "Why would not I do that today?" I concluded that I do not have the faith or the boldness that I had when I was a young man. The world has calloused and hardened me, and I do not have the closeness with the Lord that I had when I was a youngster. But the proposition I made and the gospel I was preaching that day is the truest gospel a man could preach. The invitation I extended is as true to the Word of God as any invitation a man could ever make. During these years since, having studied, I have learned why.

The Seat of Salvation

You see, the "me" that lives on the inside of this house is made up of three parts. You do not see me, you just see the house I live in. I look out at you with these two eyes. It is like this: There was an old man named Peas, and when he died, they wrote an epitaph on his tombstone which read:

> Here lies the body of old man Peas,
> Beneath the daisies and the trees.
> But Peas ain't here, only the pod,
> For Peas shelled out and gone to God.

The "me" that lives on the inside of this house is made up of three parts—my mind, my emotion, and my will or, in other words, my understanding, my feeling, and my volition. I am a tripartite creation. Of those three parts, my mind, my emotion, and my will, where is the seat of salvation? Where am I saved? Am I saved in my mind? Am I saved in my understanding? Am I saved by being smart or being educated?

We Are Not Saved in Our Minds

Would to God that we were saved in our minds. Then all we would have to do to save the world would be to send people to school. We would educate everyone into the kingdom of heaven. But just the opposite obtains.

My impression of education is that it is increasingly god-less and moves away from the Lord. The most cultured, educated, and literate of all the nations that ever existed was Nazi Germany.

In my day as a youth, if a student went to a great university in order to receive the most highly acclaimed education, he went to one of the universities in Germany. Yet, with all the culture, literacy, education, and academic achievement of the German people, there never was a people more brutal, more calloused, and more inhumane then was demonstrated in the culture, government, society, and education of Nazi Germany.

I have stood in concentration camps such as Dachau and have relived how German scientists took their prisoners and used them as guinea pigs in order to have live specimens to experiment with the human body, especially as it pertained to the machine of war.

A man is not saved because he is smart, and he is not saved because he is educated. He is not saved because he has been to school. He is not saved because he has degrees after his name. He is not saved in his mind and understanding.

We Are Not Saved in Our Feelings or Emotions

If a man is not saved in his mind, then exactly where is the seat of salvation. Is a man saved in his feeling, in his emotion? Is a man saved because he thinks he is saved and he feels that he is saved?

When I was a youngster, I was taught the James Lange theory of emotions, and I believe it to this day. If one cannot prove it, he cannot disprove it. The James Lange theory of emotions is this: emotion or feeling is nothing other than a concomitant, a summary of all the anatomical changes in your body. Everything that is going on in your body combined is your emotion, your feeling. Consequently, feelings go up and down because the anatomical changes in your body go up and down. One can scientifically graph the up and the down feelings in your body because it follows a pattern every month. They also say that if one is down all the time, he is afflicted with melancholia. If one is up all the time, he is an idot. If one is normal, he is up and down. All feelings and emotions are like that; they go up and down.

The experience of love is an emotion, a feeling, and it goes up and down. I one time heard a fellow say that he loved his wife one day so much he could eat her up. The next day he wished he had done it!

The emotions in our religious life are like the old Negro spiritual:

I'm sometimes up and I'm sometimes down,
But still my soul am heavenly bound.

Christian emotion is like the mercury in a thermometer: it goes up and it goes down, but always *inside* the thermometer. If one ever attaches his salvation to his feelings, it will drag him to death. One day he thinks: "I am saved! I can hear the angels sing. I can touch their wings." Then the next day he thinks, "I do not believe I am saved at all. I have lost my religion." If you attach your religion to your feelings, you will live a life of absolute frustration. We are not saved in our feelings.

We Are Saved in Our Will

If a man is not saved in his head and if a man is not saved in his feelings, then where is the seat of salvation? Where is a man saved? He is saved according to what God, by inspiration, has written in this Holy Word and in this sacred Bible. A man is saved in his will, in his volition. You are saved in a great decision and commitment that you make in your life. *Ho thelon,* "Whosoever will, let him take the water of life freely." It is in a decision, it is in a commitment, it is in an avowal, it is in the acceptance of the invitation of God that we are saved. It is in his love and grace, it is in his atonement for us on the cross that we are saved. It is in our decision for Christ that we find eternal life.

One might say: "I do not understand. How could God place all of the eternal destiny of the soul in one decision that a man makes?" The whole turn of life is like that. One is changed by a decision that he makes, and that decision is the difference between heaven and hell.

The Prodigal Son

Let me show you. No one can tell a story to illustrate a deep, spiritual truth as the Lord Jesus. This is the story from his blessed and holy lips. He said that there was a boss man, a ranchman in West Texas. He was the father of two sons. One day the younger son came to the father and said: "Dad, I am tired of this place! Every time I go out and get drunk, you give me a lecture. Every time I stay out beyond a certain hour, when I come back, Mom tries to convert me. Then you take me to church on Sunday. I am tired of the whole thing. Dad, I want you to give me whatever inheritance is coming to me and I am heading West."

The father pled with his boy, but to no avail. You cannot keep a boy if you do not have his heart. So the father divided with the younger son what was coming to him and the boy went on his way. You should have seen him. He bought a ten-gallon hat, new boots with golden spurs, and a palomino pony with a silver bridle.

He bought the most expensive saddle that money could buy, and when he hit town, everybody knew he was there. He lived it up in riotous living.

Back home at the table the mother sat looking at the plate. The dad said to her, "Mamma, why are not you eating?"

She said, "I am not hungry."

The father said, "Mother, what is the matter?"

She said, "Oh, nothing."

The father said: "Something is the matter. You are not eating. Why not are you eating?"

She said, "Dad, if you must know, I was just thinking about our boy."

That evening on the veranda, in the twilight of the setting sun, the father doubled up a big fist and wiped a tear out of his eye. He did not think she saw.

But the mother turned to her husband and said, "Dad, why are you crying?"

"I am not crying," he said.

"Dad, I saw you wipe a tear out of your eye. Why are you crying?"

He replied, "Mother, if you just have to know, I was thinking about our boy."

The boy had a great time for awhile. Then the day came, and it inevitably comes, when his money was gone. His friends were gone. Gone his palomino pony. Gone his golden spurs. Gone his silver bridle. Hungry, he sat on the top of a corral fence watching the hogs eat. He was so starved, he wanted to eat what they were eating, the husks for the swine. As he sat on the top of that corral fence, he began to think about home, about Mom, about Dad, and about the things of his Christian home. Tears began to fall off of his face.

As he sat there thinking about home, wretched and

miserable, an old cowpoke passed by. He looked at the boy with the tears falling off of his face and said, "Son, why are you crying?"

The boy said, "I ain't crying."

The cowpoke said, "What is the matter with you, Son?"

The boy said, "There ain't nothing wrong with me."

The cowpoke said: "Son, there is something wrong. I see the streaks in the dirt on your face where the tears have fallen down. What is the matter, Son?"

The boy replied, "If you just must know, I was thinking about home."

The old cowpoke said, "Son, do you have a home somewhere?"

The boy said, "Yes, sir."

The cowpoke said: "Son, I one time had a Christian home, and I broke the heart of my father and mother. They are in heaven now. I wish I could go back. Son, if you have a Christian father and mother somewhere, you go back." The old cowpoke sauntered away.

As the boy sat on the top of the corral fence, he said: "I will. I will go back to my father and home."

And, oh, the heavenly scene that followed after!

When the father saw him coming, he ran, embraced him, kissed him, and said, "Bring the finest robe that we have. Take off those rags and clothe him with scarlet. Take the insignia ring of heirship and kinship and put it on his finger. Kill the fatted calf and let us feast and rejoice, for this my son was dead and is alive again. He was lost and now he is found!"

From whence did all that arise! It came from a sentence, from a simple decision, "I will."

Is not that exactly what is in the Book? "And whosoever will, let him take the water of life freely." When a man says "I will" to God, God does something. When a child, when a youth, when a girl, when a woman, when a boy says that sentence, "I will," God does the rest. He is the one who saves. He is the one who regenerates. He is the one who writes our name in the Book of Life. All we have to do is to receive his grace. "I will," and I am saved. "I will," and Jesus does the rest!

15.

The Harvest Is Past

When I would comfort myself against sorrow, my heart is faint in me.

Behold the voice of the cry of the daughter of my people because of them that dwell in a far country: Is not the Lord in Zion? is not her king in her? Why have they provoked me to anger with their graven images, and with strange vanities?

The harvest is past, the summer is ended and we are not saved.

For the hurt of the daughter of my people am I hurt; I am black; astonishment hath taken hold on me.

Is there no balm in Gilead: is there no physician there? why then is not the health of the daughter of my people recovered?

Oh that my head were waters, and mine eyes a fountain of tears, that I might weep day and night for the slain of the daughter of my people!" (Jer. 8:18–22; 9:1).

There is no sorrow in all the Word of God more poignantly expressed than the cry of the prophet in Jeremiah 8:20, "The harvest is past, the summer is ended, and we are not saved."

Everything Mundane Has an End

All things, if they are mundane and terrestrial, somewhere, sometime have an end. They have an ultimate and final conclusion. There is never a river so long but that somewhere it loses itself in the vast and illimitable expanse of the sea. There is never a day that blushes at the dawn rising to noonday, meridian strength but that dies in the twilight and shades of the night. There is never a year that comes to the birth in the spring, that fruits and flowers in the summer, but that dies, perishes in the cold of the winter. So is our life. We spend it as a tale that is told. I know the end from the beginning. We shall certainly fall into death.

One time I stood in the giant Sequoia National Park in California looking at the tall redwood trees, great in girth and greater in age. Some of those trees are said to have been a thousand years old when Jesus was born. As I marveled at their height and breadth, by the side of those standing giants I saw other Sequoia trees, equally as tall, equally as great, equally as big, equally as old, lying prostrate and decaying in the soil of the ground. All things somewhere sometime have their end. It is thus with our lives. Our day of grace, our day of opportunity is so brief and it soon passes away.

One time one of my deacons came to me and said: "Pastor, next door to me has moved a family. I visited with them. They are all lost. Not one of them is a Christian. Would you come and tell them how to be saved?"

I went to the home, knocked at the door, and was graciously invited in. I met a father, a mother, a boy about sixteen, a girl about seventeen, and another boy about twelve. I talked to them about Jesus. They were so responsive and said, "Preacher, next Sunday we will be in church." When the services began, I looked over the throng. They were not present. I waited about two or three weeks and went back to the home. I talked to them again about the Lord. They said: "Pastor, we shall be there next Sunday. We shall certainly come to church." The Sunday came and they were not there.

The following week in the wee hours of the morning, I received a telephone call from a nurse in our Baptist hospital who belonged to our church. She said: "Pastor, with great reluctance do I call you at this hour of the morning, but there is a boy in the hospital who has been grievously hurt. The boy has just a few hours to live. His father is standing by his side, and I asked him if there was anybody that he knew who might stand by him in this tragic moment. He said that he knows you. I just wondered if you would come and stand by his side when his boy dies?"

I dressed, went to the hospital room where the boy was lying prostrate, terribly crushed in an automobile accident. The boy had been driving furiously back into the city and had a head-on collision. Standing above him was his father. I took my place by his side, just standing there looking at that broken boy. In just a little while the nurse took the white sheet and pulled it over the boy's face. She looked at the father and said, "Your boy is gone." She left the room.

After the nurse had left, the father pulled the sheet away from the face of that boy. Looking long and silently into his face, the father fell down on the floor. By the side of the bed, he began to cry unconsolably: "O my God, my boy is gone, and I have not lived right before him. I have not done right by him. O God, what shall I do?"

After the memorial service and the boy was buried away, down the aisle in the church the following Sunday morning came the father, the mother, the seventeen-year-old girl, and the twelve-year-old boy. When the benediction was over, the people who were shaking hands with me said: "Pastor was not that the most glorious

sight in the world? The whole family was won to Jesus—
the father, mother, daughter, and son. All of them were
saved!"

I said, "Yes, that was a glorious sight." But in my
heart as I looked at them seated there on the front seat,
I said: "This is the saddest sight in the world. Would
to God they had come a week before!"

Someday when they stand at the judgment bar of the
Almighty and the roll is called in heaven, God will call
the name of the father and he will answer, "Here." God
will call the name of the mother and she will answer,
"Here." He will call the name of the seventeen-year-
old girl and she will answer, "Here." He will call the
name of the twelve-year-old boy and he will answer,
"Here." Then the Lord God shall look into the face of
the father and say, "Is that all?"

The father will answer: "No. We have another boy
sixteen years of age."

The Lord shall ask, "Where is he?"

The father will reply, "My boy lies in a Christless
grave in Texas tonight."

"The harvest is past, the summer is ended, and we
are not saved" (Jer. 8:20). Our time and our opportunities
are so fleeting, so brief, and so swiftly passing. My day
of grace is just now.

Everything Is Moving Toward the Final Consummation

We all are hastening to that great and final assize, the
judgment day of Almighty God. Scientists say that our
entire galaxy and the vast universe of which our earth
is a part is all moving furiously through space, going
where? Somewhere to a rendezvous where we shall meet
Almighty God. History in which our very lives are inex-

tricably bound is moving rapidly through time towards a great rendezvous with Almighty God, to the judgment day of the Lord. However our paths may divert in this life, we shall all appear some day at the judgment bar of Almighty God. A little babe in the cradle, reaching up his tiny arms, is reaching for the judgment day of Almighty God. A youth, striding by with elastic tread, is moving toward the judgment day of Almighty God. The old man with his crutch and his cane is tottering toward the judgment day of Almighty God. The rich man, riding in his splendid automobile, is riding toward the judgment day of Almighty God. The poor man in tatters and bare feet is walking to the judgment day of Almighty God.

The Christian with songs on his lips and with praises in his heart is pilgrimaging to the great judgment day of Almighty God. The lost man, doing despite to the Spirit of grace and treading under foot the blood of the covenant wherewith he was sanctified, is marching toward the great judgment day of Almighty God. Someday we shall all appear before the Lord God who made us to give an account for the days of our flesh. Then shall come the great separation.

One time I heard as a youth an old, white-headed, retired preacher in the southern part of Indiana describing the years of his ministry. He also described the times that he had presided over a memorial service and had listened to a wife weep over the face of her dead husband, crying, "Good-bye, good-bye," or a father and mother crying over the face of their child, "Good-bye, good-bye." Then he added: "That is not good-bye. That is just "Farewell," that is just "Till I see you again." For they will meet again at the judgment. Oh, the sadness of that final separation if one is lost!

The Great Separation

Our Lord said more about the judgment day and the traumatic separation that will come to pass than about any other thing in the life of his ministry. Sometimes he would describe it as wheat and tares, one gathered into the garner and the other burned with unquenchable fire. Sometimes he would describe it as a shepherd divides his sheep from the goats. Sometimes he would describe it as a fisherman gathering in the nets, choosing the good, casting away the bad. Sometimes he would describe it as a bridal evening, when the five wise virgins enter in and the five foolish virgins are closed out. Sometimes he described it as a great gulf fixed between the lost and the saved. Then I can hear someone say: "But that is just theology. That is just preaching. That is just something that a preacher conjures up or an interpretation he makes to frighten us and to scare us."

Not so. I know of nothing in this life that is more poignantly and tragically true than the great abyss between the lost and the saved, between those who lift up their faces toward heaven and those whose faces are buried in the thoughts and the life of this world.

One time on the wrong side of the railroad tracks, one of my deacons was holding a revival meeting. I went over to a morning service to encourage and help him. He did something that morning that I have never seen before. He started in the back of the congregation and asked each one, "Do you have a burden on your heart?" When someone replied, "Yes, I have a burden on my heart," the deacon would say, "What is the burden on your heart?" The person would reply and describe his burden. Then the deacon would say, "Let us all bow our heads and you lead the prayer. We will all pray with you for your burden."

Seated directly in front of me sat a little mother who had a baby in her arms and a little boy just old enough to play on the bench by her side. The deacon came to her and said, "Little mother, is there a burden on your heart?"

She said, "Yes."

He asked, "What is the burden on your heart?"

She replied, "Oh, that my husband might be saved, that he might be a Christian!"

The deacon said, "We will all bow our heads and pray, and little mother, you lead the prayer that God will save your husband."

So we all bowed our heads. We waited for the little mother to pray that God would save her husband. As we waited, she just began to cry. She did not say anything. As we continued to wait, she began to sob aloud, weeping unconsolably. So I stood up and said, "Deacon, if you do not mind, let me pray in her stead."

He said, "Pastor, yes. You lead the prayer."

I prayed for her husband, wherever he was, that he might be saved, that he might come to know the Lord.

After my prayer, I sat down. But while I had prayed, the little boy, who was just old enough to play on the pew by her side, had worked himself up into his mother's arms. Looking directly into her face, wide-eyed and innocent, he asked, "Mu-va, whatcha cryin' for?"

The mother did not answer.

The little boy pressed his appeal. "Mu-va, whatcha cryin' for?"

The mother never replied. She never answered. Seated right behind her, I could look directly into the wide-

opened eyes of that little boy. As I looked into his eyes,
I said within my heart: "Sonny lad, you are too young
to know why your mother cries, but someday you will.
She will be in church and Dad will be out in the world.
Your mother will be praying to God and reading the
Holy Scriptures and your father will be enmeshed in the
things of the world. The day will come when the angels
will carry the soul of Mother to heaven and Daddy will
be left behind."

I know of no fact in life that is deeper or more traumatic
than the great gulf between those who are saved and
those who are lost.

> When the choir has sung its last anthem,
> And the preacher has prayed his last prayer,
> When the people have heard their last sermon,
> And the sound has died out in the air.
> When the Bible lies closed on the altar,
> And the pews are all emptied of men,
> And each one stands facing his record,
> And the great Book is opened, what then?
>
> When the actor has played his last drama,
> And the mimic has made his last fun,
> When the film has flashed its last picture,
> And the billboard displayed its last run.
>
> When the crowds seeking pleasure have vanished,
> And gone out in the darkness again,
> And the trumpet of ages is sounded,
> And we stand before Him, what then?
>
> When the bugle's call sinks into silence,
> And the long, marching columns stand still,

When the captain repeats his last orders,
And they've captured the last fort and hill.
When the flag is hauled down from the masthead,
And the wounded afield checked in,
And a world that rejected its Saviour,
Is asked for a reason, what then?

"The harvest is past, the summer is ended, and we are not saved." We have just a moment. We have just today. We have just this brief opportunity, and then our day of grace is gone.

Lord, while I have my mind, help me to make the decision for Christ. While my heart beats, may it be opened Godward and heavenward. While I have this moment, precious Jesus, give me strength to make that saving commitment to our Lord now!

16.
Spiritual Conquest . . . Now!

Rise, and stand upon thy feet: for I have appeared unto thee for this purpose, to make thee a minister and a witness both of these things which thou hast seen, and of those things in the which I will appear unto thee;

Delivering thee from the people, and from the Gentiles, unto whom now I send thee,

To open their eyes, and to turn them from darkness to light, and from the power of Satan unto God, that they may receive forgiveness of sins, and inheritance among them which are sanctified by faith that is in me.

Whereupon, O king Agrippa, I was not disobedient unto the heavenly vision:

But shewed first unto them of Damascus, and at Jerusalem, and throughout all the coasts of Judaea, and then to the Gentiles, that they should repent and turn to God, and do works meet for repentance (Acts 26:16–20).

One will find the spirit of urgency reflected in the text repeated in the words Paul wrote in 2 Corinthians 5 and 6:

> Knowing therefore the terror of the Lord, we persuade men.
>
> We are ambassadors for Christ, as though God did beseech you by us: we pray you in Christ's stead, be ye reconciled to God (5:11, 20).

We then, as workers together with him, beseech
you also that ye receive not the grace of God in
vain.

(For he saith, I have heard thee in a time accepted,
and in the day of salvation have I succoured thee:
behold, now is the accepted time; behold, now is
the day of salvation) (6:1–2).

First I speak of our world, the whole world, and our
present day of grace. We live, every citizen of every nation in the earth, as one under a Damocles sword. We
live as one with a gun pointed to his head. We live in
the woe of history, in impending judgment and certain
catastrophe. One sees this in the very titles of the name
of the chapters in modern books of history. A chapter
will be called "The Demise of Modern Civilization." Another chapter will be entitled "The Post-Christian Era."
Historians who have followed the story of the human
race from its inception to this present moment look with
dread and foreboding to the future.

I could illustrate that no better than in the first three
times I was in Germany, the first visit within a few
months after the close of the Second World War. All
of the cities that I saw in Germany were great heaps of
endless rubble. For example, standing in the heart of
Hamburg, from horizon to horizon I saw nothing but
debris, not a building standing, not a house, only vast,
endless measures of stone, stick, and destruction. The
second time that I was in Germany I went to a play, a
modern play called *Faust.* The star in the play was Orson
Welles. Over and over again there was repeated this refrain, "Damnation is contagious." Presented in the midst
of Munich which was still half destroyed, the play ended
with a clock in an atomic bomb ticking away, a play

that was presenting our modern world. The third time that I was in Germany I went to see an opera called *Die Götterdämmerung*, the last section of a trilogy written by Richard Wagner. The spear of the god Wotan is broken. Siegfried has been slain, Brunhilde casts herself upon the funeral pyre, and Valhalla is on fire. The opera ends with the dissolution of heaven and earth. These things seem to me to be portraits of the world in which we live. We have a brief time of grace before the certain judgment of Almighty God.

Our Day of Grace

Second, let us look at our nation of America, whether we live or perish. Jeremiah the prophet lifted up his voice and cried to a debauched and wayward nation, "Repent." The Babylonians came in 605 B.C. and carried away Daniel and some of the blood royal.

Jeremiah lifted up his voice and cried, "Repent." The nation continued in its own debauched way, and the Babylonians came in 598 B.C. and carried away Ezekiel and many of the priesthood and the elite of the land.

Jeremiah lifted up his voice and cried, "Repent." The Babylonians came in 587 B.C. after the nation persisted in its ungodly way, and they did not need to come again. They destroyed the nation, carried the people into captivity, burned the holy city with fire, and destroyed the Solomonic temple forever.

I liken the encounter of 605 B.C. to the First World War, the encounter in 598 B.C. to the Second World War, and we stand now in ominous dread and foreboding of the third and final world war. When we fight this next confrontation with atomic weapons, we will live to see a world of endless, immeasurable, and indescribable destruction. You see, I cannot believe that America in

drunkenness, disobedience, disgrace, desecration, and debauchery can survive. Still written in the Word of God
is, "The wicked shall be turned into hell, and all the
nations that forget God" (Ps. 9:17). The rising graph of
crime in America is beyond that of any nation on the
face of the globe and we are becoming increasingly anti-
Christ and anti-God and anti-church.

> Far-called, our navies melt away;
> On dune and headland sinks of fire;
> Lo, all our pomp of yesterday
> Is one with Ninevah and Tyre!
> Judge of the Nations, spare us yet,
> Lest we forget—lest we forget!

RUDYARD KIPLING

In every national conflict and confrontation that America has ever known and ever had, we have been under
the guiding, protecting hand of Almighty God. Whether
the Lord will protect us in the future lies in those impon-
derables known but to him. Heaven grant that we may
not be weighed in the balances and found wanting.

Our Denomination—Whether We Live or Die

Next I speak of our faith, our communion, and our
denomination. There are in America toward one hundred
million people who belong to no church whatsoever. Do
you think that that spiritual vacuum will continue? No.
Someone will win their hearts, their minds, their loyalties,
their faith, and their trust.

I remember reading in history of the Unitarian defection that emptied the churches of New England, in the

land of our great Protestant, pilgrim fathers. Did that Unitarian defection that emptied the churches of New England create a permanent vacuity and void? No. The Roman Catholic church today boasts that it can present a solid Catholic vote in New England.

This in the land of our pilgrim fathers.

This in the land of the Great Awakening under George Whitefield and Johnathan Edwards.

This in the land of the great revivals under Charles G. Finney and Dwight L. Moody.

The most solidly Catholic city in America is Providence and the most solidly Catholic state in the Union is Rhode Island, the state which was founded by our great Baptist progenitor, Roger Williams, and kept faithful to the word by John Clark. The unchurched will not remain in a spiritual vacuum; someone will win them, either we or someone else.

When Alexander the Great lay dying, his generals standing by his bed asked, "Whose is the kingdom?" Having no heir, Alexander replied, "It is for him who can take it."

> Bring me my bow of burning gold,
> Bring me my arrows of desire,
> Bring me my spear, O clouds unfold,
> Bring me my chariot of fire.

> We shall not cease from battle strife
> Nor shall the sword sleep in our hand,
> 'Til we have built Jerusalem
> In this fair and pleasant land.

—WILLIAM BLAKE

Our denomination, whether we live or die, and the
lost of our people, whether they are saved or perish without Christ, is determined by whether we care or are filled
with vast, abysmal indifference. "O that my head were
waters . . . that I might weep day and night for the . . .
daughter of my people!" (Jer. 9:1). The compassionate
heart that seeks after these who know not Christ as a
living Savior is our present greatest need.

In a book that I read, a philosopher is seated in the
great Roman Colosseums and he is watching the gladiato-
rial combat on the sand in the center arena. As those
men speared and battled one another to the death, and
as the sand was stained with the red crimson blood of
life, the philosopher turns to his friend and says, "What
is needed is the heart that would make it impossible to
look upon such suffering and bloodshed and the future
would belong to the power that could create that heart."
He did not know it, but he was describing the compassionate, loving care of the Christian faith, the heart of
which goes out in behalf of the salvation of all men everywhere. There is no substitute for the compassionate heart,
the Spirit of the Lord Jesus that loves and cares, that
yearns over the lost.

A young preacher who died in his twenties made one
of the greatest impressions upon Scotland of any preacher
who ever lived. A visitor came from afar to see the secret
of the young man. The preacher was not there, only the
caretaker. When the caretaker learned why the man had
come, the caretaker said, "Come with me." He took him
to the study of the young preacher and said, "This is
his chair in which he studies and this is the desk on
which he places his books; sit in his chair." The man
sat in the chair. Then the caretaker said, "Now put your
hands on the top of the desk." The visitor put his hands

on the top of the desk, and the caretaker said, "Now bury your face in your hands and weep."

This is a facet, an element, and an integral part of the Christian faith that, if it is ever taken away, the faith becomes dust and ashes in our hands. We must have a burdened heart, a face that knows tears, and the prayer that the lost might be saved. We have many assignments, but our first and primary assignment always is the ministry of the blessed saving knowledge of Christ to the lost.

> You have builded temples in His name
> Of mortar and brick and stone,
> With windows of glass most beautifully stained
> With steeple and spire and dome.
>
> But what do we of the by-ways care
> For structure and line and trim?
> Out in the dust of the lonely road
> We only ask for Him.
>
> You have robed your choirs and trained them well
> In proper and intricate song.
> You have bought fine organs to edify
> And lulled the weary throng.
>
> But what do we care for your black-robed choir
> Or your organ's deep "A-men"?
> We want you to walk beside us here
> And point the way to Him.
>
> Oh, the roads of the world are a crooked maze
> And we are woefully lost,
> For the road to Him in the paths of men
> Is faint and hidden and crossed.

What do we care for the trappings of art
When our hearts' high hope is dim?
We seek the touch of His healing hand
Oh, show us the way to Him.

—Author Unknown

This is the great assignment of the church. This is the great prerogative of the minister of Christ, and this is the sharing of the gospel message of everyone who has found faith, hope, salvation, and life in him that others also might come to know the Lord, whom to know is life in this world and in the world that is to come. God bless us as a people, as leaders, as followers, as teachers, as disciples, as learners that we exhibit to the world a heart that is full of love, care, and prayers that bombard the throne of grace in heaven that the lost might be saved and the name of Christ might be honored in the hearts of men.